JOURNEY ROUND St HELIER

Front cover: the author in the Royal Square
Back cover: the author returning from Elizabeth Castle
Both photographs by Sarah McClelland

The Town Church

JOURNEY ROUND St HELIER

*Six strolls discovering people and places
in the town at the centre of Jersey's affairs*

Robin Pittman

(Author of *Hotel: West of Albert*, *Speaking of Jersey*,
Journey Round Jersey and *Journey Across Jersey*)

Foreword by Simon Crowcroft, Connétable of St Helier

Illustrations by David Barlow

SEAFLOWER BOOKS

Published in 2009 by
SEAFLOWER BOOKS
16A St John's Road
St Helier
Jersey
JE2 3LD

Origination by Seaflower Books

Printed by Cromwell Press Group
Trowbridge, Wiltshire

Typeset in 10/13 Plantin

ISBN 978-1-906641-12-2

© 2009 Robin Pittman (text)
© 2009 David Barlow (illustrations)
© 2009 Sarah McClelland (front & back cover photographs)
© 2009 AEA Design Ltd. (maps)

Contents

	Foreword by Simon Crowcroft, Connétable of St Helier	7
	Introduction	9
1	**The Royal Square to Elizabeth Castle by way of the Esplanade and the Waterfront**	11
	Sir Philip Bailhache, Matthew Chase, Rod McLoughlin, Graham and Pauline Cooper, Heather Brown, David de Carteret, Maria da Silva, Paul Le Brocq, John Noel, Captain Howard Le Cornu, Stuart Johnson, Marc Tollamore, Sonia Rodrigues, Adrian de St George, Shaun McKernan, Elaine Rabet, Christine Holmes, Ted Clucas, Deborah Caeres, Andy Errington-Rennell, Angela Trigg, Jon Troy, Ian and Kathleen Hughes, David Coom	
2	**The Royal Square and up Rouge Bouillon by way of King Street and The Parade**	38
	Andy, Gerald Voisin, Cartia, Peter Noble, David Mashiter, Jasmine Hendry, Mike Pollard, Pamela Eugenio, Martin, Robert, Paul, Jackie Edwards, Manuel Alfonso, Isabel Cerca, Roger Bara, John Moulin, Colin Belsey, Andrew Moisan, Paul Okumu	
3	**The Royal Square to Almorah Crescent by way of New Street, Union Street, Halkett Place, Val Plaisant and Midvale Road**	66
	Colin Smith, Antony Gibb, Ernie Le Brun, Tristan Lewis, Bill Ogley, David Le Heuzé, Anna Brzozowski, James Garvie, Pat Davis, William Philpott, Gary Bisson, Sheelah Langlois, Reverend Liz Hunter, Monsignor Nicholas France, Nancy Murphy, Norma Parkinson, Mrs Hales-Coleman, Bernard Morris, Alex Bosnovic	
4	**The Royal Square to Windsor Crescent by way of the Market, David Place and Stopford Road**	92

Greg Collenette, John Farley, John Le Saint, Billy Davies, Richard MacKenzie, John Hunter, Daniel Austin, Advocate Christopher Lakeman, Deputy Kevin Lewis, Isabella Lewis, Dennis Perrin, Stephen Dunford, Clive Barton

5	**The Royal Square to Victoria College by way of Morier House, Green Street and St Saviour's Road** Michael de la Haye, Emma Martins, Shaun Rankin, Linda Romeril, Dr Rosemary Geller, Major Stephen Coleman, Chris Beirne, Naomi Garton, Callum Gillies	115
6	**The Royal Square to Fort Regent by way of Commercial Buildings, La Collette and Havre des Pas** Deputy Montfort Tadier, Alcino Vieira, Carlos Mogueira, Ovalerie Wendiady, Jon Carter, Frank McFarland, Christopher Fairbairn, Terry Amy, David Knight, Peter Gully, Emily Moore, Angie Boucheré, Senator Freddie Cohen	138

Foreword

by Simon Crowcroft, Connétable of St Helier

The journey on foot is the oldest form of travel and the account of a pedestrian tour one of the oldest literary forms; and well before travellers were able to set down an account of their journey on paper, they would of course have wanted to leave an oral record to be passed from village to village and re-told, no doubt with much alteration and exaggeration, around the camp-fires of far-away settlements. Robin Pittman's latest book completing, as he says in his introduction, a trilogy recording his walks around Jersey, takes its place in the long and varied bibliography of travel writing about the Channel Islands and provides a useful addition to it.

Journey Round St Helier appears at a particularly appropriate juncture in the history of Jersey's main town; the burgeoning financial services industry and the steady rise of immigration have transformed the town's topography in the last half-century. As Islanders consider how to protect what remains of Jersey's unspoilt rural and coastal areas, attention is increasingly being focused on St Helier as the place in which to construct the thousands of new homes that will be required in the next few decades. The majority of these homes will of course have to be created in the form of apartments – unless people wish to see the Island become suburbs from shore to shore. A key question will therefore be whether the States of Jersey is willing to compensate these apartment dwellers for the absence of private gardens and garages and for the other quality of life issues such as noise, traffic fumes and the like, with improved public transport systems, safe routes for cyclists and pedestrians, affordable leisure and cultural facilities and ample space in the form of parks, gardens and squares.

As our guide pursues his half-dozen walks from the Royal Square, we are shown the juxtaposition of the old and new, both in terms of the built fabric and in the human encounters that provide the backbone to all of Robin Pittman's Journey accounts. It is striking how many of the Islanders and visitors interviewed in the course of this book have positive things to say about the state of St Helier. This is especially true of more recent additions to the townscape which tend to be unloved by locals. The bus station for example, according to a visiting bus driver (who should know), 'beats anything in the UK', while the Radisson Hotel on the Waterfront is reckoned to have the best views of more than 400 hotels around the world. As somewhere to live St Helier is described by one contributor as 'a special

FOREWORD ~

place, one that does not empty in the evenings when the financiers get in their company cars and drive away to the rural parishes. So many people live within half a mile of the Market and this is one of the reasons why it continues to be such an important and lively retail centre'.

Anyone who explores the major towns of Normandy, especially St Helier's twin town, Avranches, cannot help but notice the destruction of so much *patrimoine* during the Second World War and particularly during the battles that followed the D-day landings. A visitor to St Helier could be forgiven for thinking that our town was also subjected to aerial bombardment, given the loss of such buildings as FCJ Convent in Val Plaisant and the destruction of most of Hue Street, and the host of others the demise of which is recorded in André Ferrari's books, *Jersey's Lost Heritage: Fifty years of needless destruction* (1996) and *Jersey's Disappearing Heritage: Fifty years of neglect* (1998).

Yet just as the human histories and perspectives on St Helier are predominantly upbeat, so there is still much to celebrate in our main town's built fabric. Robin Pittman takes as his chief vade mecum C.E.B. Brett's *Buildings in the Town and Parish of St Helier*, long out of print. One of the special pleasures of Robin's book is that it reminds us of the majority of architectural delights that St Helier still affords to the walker and provides useful introductions to them. No doubt a lot of people will be seen following in his footsteps in the coming years with a well-used if not battered copy of *Journey Round St Helier* in their hand and noting the changes that will have taken place on his half-dozen chosen routes. We can only hope that the majority of changes will be beneficial.

Introduction

When my *Journey Round Jersey* was published in 2005, a kind reviewer suggested that there could be two sequels, *Journey Across Jersey* and *Journey Round St Helier*. The former appeared in 2007 and, with the publication of this book, it is a case of 'mission accomplished'.

This is not a comprehensive guide to the architecture of St Helier. Instead it is six walks, all of them beginning in and fanning out from the Royal Square, with buildings noted and many people, living and working in the town, encountered and engaged in conversation. The routes taken are, for the most part, within the ring road, with forays outside it to Elizabeth Castle, Almorah Crescent, Victoria College and a few other venues that lie beyond the area bounded by Rouge Bouillon and St Saviour's Road.

Two books have proved of immense help to me. The first is *Buildings in the Town and Parish of St Helier* by C.E.B. Brett, published in 1977, and the other is *Architecture in Jersey* by Maurice Boots, sometime Chief States Architect, and published in 1986. I have quoted extensively from the former and have also valued comments contained in the latter. Brett's survey is the closest we have in Jersey to a volume in Nikolaus Pevsner's *The Buildings of England* series. Might it now be opportune for Jersey, including St Helier, to have its own 'Pevsner', perhaps a commission to be undertaken by the Société Jersiaise?

Brett has some wise words to say about St Helier in his introduction. They are worth quoting:

> It is not at first sight a particularly attractive town; nor is it one of very obvious architectural distinction. Brash and ill-considered multi-storey buildings of the post-war years have unduly intruded on such unity of style and scale as it once possessed. Yet…St Helier retains a surprising number of individual buildings and groups of merit and significance. It is a town which tends to hide its lights under bushels; though there is not much to excite the flâneur who wanders casually around its centre, the visitor who is prepared to explore side-alleys and half-suburban avenues will find some unexpected rewards.

I hope that my *Journey Round St Helier* may cast a light on both the architecture of the town at the centre of the Island's affairs and on the lives and employment of some of those, both important and less so, whose work or circumstances have

INTRODUCTION ~

brought them to this place.

I owe thanks to several people whose help has been considerable: to Simon Crowcroft, Connétable of St Helier, for his foreword, to Alan Eaton of AEA Design Ltd for the maps, to Sarah McClelland for the cover photographs, to David Barlow for his illustrations, to Mike Good for his eagle eye in spotting grammatical and other infelicities, to Roger Jones of Seaflower Books and as ever to my wife for her proof-reading and continual support and love.

RNP, St Mary, Jersey, November 2009

1

The Royal Square to Elizabeth Castle by way of the Esplanade and the Waterfront

The Royal Square seemed the appropriate place for the start of my journey round St Helier as I stood on the stone in the middle of this well-paved promenade with its brief carved inscription:

> The Battle of Jersey was fought in the Royal Square
> formerly the Market Place
> on the sixth of January 1781

Indeed this was the original market place of the town until 1803. C.E.B. Brett in his *Buildings in the Town and Parish of St Helier* describes the Square as 'charming, irregularly shaped, a whole whose merits are greater than the sum of its parts'. It may be true that none of its buildings is of special architectural merit, but here surely we are at the very heart of St Helier, indeed of the Island of Jersey.

The Royal Square is closed to the south by the range of States Buildings, and Brett, not attracted by their architectural quality, is worth quoting again: 'It is wholly satisfactory neither in mass, silhouette, colour, texture, shape nor detail: it is uncomfortably like an ancient aircraft-carrier run aground by accident in the Royal Square. Yet it undoubtedly commands the affection of the citizens, who like the Royal Square exactly as it is'.

As I stood taking in Brett's reservations, I gave more than a passing glance at the statue of George II, gilded lead, slightly less than life-size and with His Majesty dressed as a Roman senator. It was erected with much pomp and circumstance in 1751 and gave the square its name. Also I reflected on that battle of 1781: Baron de Rullecourt marching from La Rocque with his forces through the night into St Helier and the Square and then being successfully challenged by the young Major Peirson commanding British troops and the Jersey Militia, with the victorious Peirson and the vanquished de Rullecourt dying in the mêlée and both

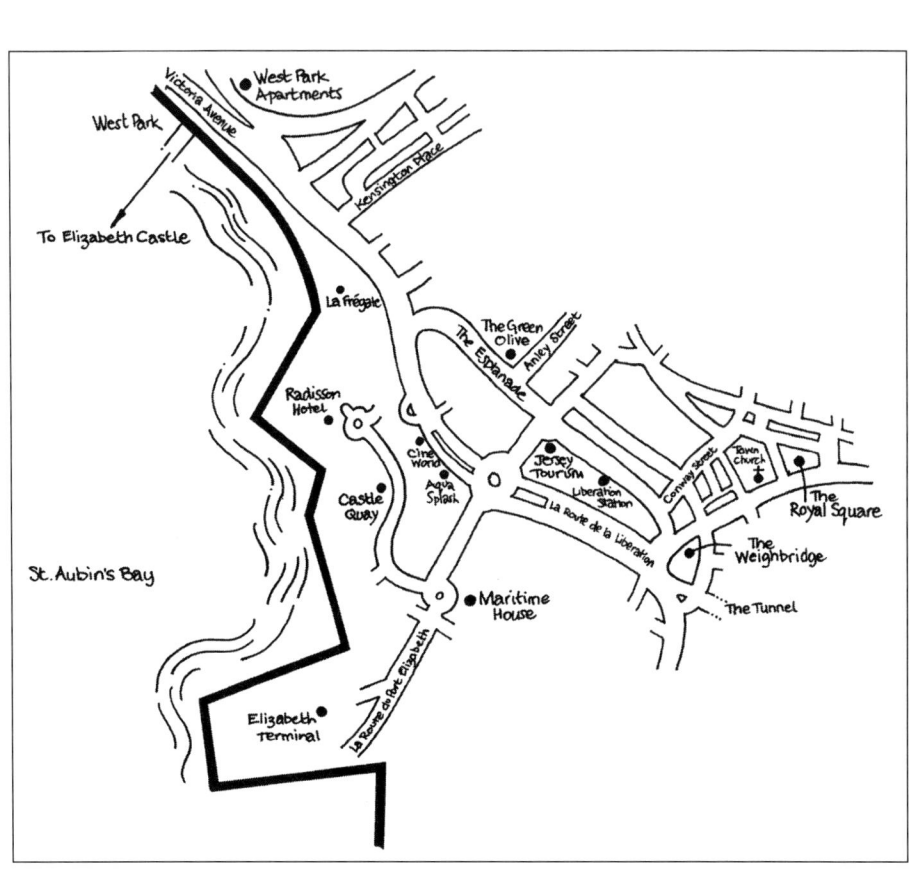

subsequently buried in the Town Church nearby.

I thought it appropriate at the start of my journey round St Helier and at the very heart of its institutions of government to meet the Island's then Bailiff, Sir Philip Bailhache, shortly before his retirement. Slightly tense with expectation I climbed the stairs to the Bailiff's Chambers and was ushered in to Sir Philip's presence by a secretary. The Bailiff came to greet me from behind his large desk and we sat down at a large glass-topped table in this imposing room, indicative of its occupant's high office, with its impressive shelves of legal tomes and with the Town Church across the road outside and visible through its windows.

Sir Philip first told me something of his early life and education: Jersey-born in 1946 and educated at Charterhouse and then, some years behind me, at my own Oxford college, Pembroke, where he read Law. Called to the bar in London, he then came back to the family law firm (with his father about to retire and to become a Jurat). Crown appointments followed: Solicitor-General in 1975, Attorney-General in 1986, Deputy Bailiff in 1994 and Bailiff the following year.

I asked Sir Philip if he would describe his role. 'It has, I suppose, three elements: the judicial, the parliamentary and the civic. The Bailiff is chief justice, presiding over the Royal Court and President of the Court of Appeal. My parliamentary function derives from presidency of the States Assembly, and the role of civic head of the Island devolves from the Bailiff carrying out that function.' Was there, I asked, any conflict from his being both the chief judge and also 'Speaker' of the States? 'I think not; theoretically it may be seen as problematic, but the dual role does not give rise to any significant difficulties. It is perfectly possible to preside over the States and act in a quasi-judicial capacity in maintaining order. Remember, I have no political role; I don't make political decisions; I have no political power; I cannot vote; indeed the Bailiff's casting vote was removed in 2005; I speak in the States only to keep order.'

I then asked Sir Philip how the role of Bailiff has changed over the last half-century or more. 'Coutanche during the Occupation was in effect the chief executive, chairing the Superior Council and very much in charge,' he responded. 'Since then his successors have distanced themselves from the political process, and it is fair to say that the Bailiff nowadays has no political authority at all. There is perhaps some influence that attaches to the office simply because it is an ancient one. But there is no power.' I then pointed out that Sir Philip had made clear his opposition to the December 2000 Clothier Report which recommended radical changes to Jersey's machinery of government and political system. Had he been right to intervene in this way? His response was robust: 'It was one of those circumstances where I would have been criticised whether I had spoken out or whether I had kept silent. Some of Clothier's recommendations were fundamental to the way that the Island is run and it was necessary to challenge the review panel's thinking. It was a nicely written and packaged report but it failed to give the underlying reasons for the recommendations being made.'

I then moved on to asking the Bailiff about Jersey's relationship with the United Kingdom. Was it true that it was more comfortable for both Jersey and the UK if these links were not too clearly defined? 'Yes, there are different ideas of what the constitutional relationship is, and in any time of crisis these conflicting perceptions necessarily surface.' Sir Philip then added: 'It is my own view, and a personal one, that we ought to be thinking of considering independence - sovereign status for the Island.' I was further jolted when he added, 'I should not be surprised were Jersey to be an independent state in fifty years' time.'

We then discussed Sir Philip's long involvement in the Island's arts, instrumental with others in founding the Arts Centre in 1983 and more recently chairing the working party developing plans for a national gallery. 'As a community we have invested quite a lot in the performing arts – the Arts Centre, the Opera House and St James's – but so far the fine arts have to some extent been neglected. We need somewhere to display the Island collection and things are moving positively here.'

I ended by asking the Bailiff to tell me his thoughts about Jersey's future. 'I hope that we can become a little more self-confident, more conscious of our history and heritage. We already have a wonderful society: geographical beauty, our own little historic idiosyncrasies, an interesting mix of population with its different national groupings. I want to encourage the notion of a small nation, with differences of origin forgotten and a people with a combined loyalty to the Island that is their home.'

I had one last thrust: federation with Guernsey? 'Possibly,' was the reply. 'We are two small islands in a somewhat hostile sea. We should be doing more things in common but there has to be the political will. I think that this political will in at least one of the islands is not perhaps as strong as it could be.' After that rather elliptical remark, I asked Sir Philip whether he had anything more which he would like me to record. 'No,' he replied with a chuckle, 'I have probably sunk myself already.'

~

I descended the stairs from the Bailiff's Chambers and left the Royal Square and all its associations with Jersey's judicial and political arrangements and made for the Town Church across the road. It is essentially a 14th century building incorporating remains of earlier work and, like so many other medieval Anglican churches, very substantially restored in the mid-Victorian period. Perhaps the handsome railings are worth more than a glance; Brett informs us that they were erected in 1845 to designs by none other than Jersey's 'J.W.M. Turner', local artist Jean Le Capelain. Without going overboard, Brett also describes the church as 'a pleasing building of reddish granite'. He is much less happy, and rightly so, with Church House that lies on the north side of the churchyard. It was built in 1969 and its fussy, fidgety design and grey granite make it an unhappy modern relation of its ancient and imposing neighbour.

I wandered through the church's north door, protected by a 15th century porch, into the empty nave, picked up an informative laminated leaflet and took in some of the features which I was invited to note. In front of the chancel steps is the tomb of Major Peirson, hero of the 1781 Battle of Jersey. Above is the fine vaulting that supports the bell chamber of the 15th century tower. In the choir some exposed stones are said once to have been part of 11th century Norman window arches. The inscription on one window reminds us of the Le Breton family, with the Very Reverend William Corbet Le Breton being not only Dean and Rector from 1875 to 1888 but also the father of Lillie Langtry (about whom little more by way of explanation needs to be said).

As I was mooching around, a relatively young man with a cheerful and welcoming manner came in and interrupted my ecclesiastical sightseeing reveries. He greeted me and we sat down in a convenient pew. I discovered that I was talking to Matthew Chase, the Town Church's verger and town centre missioner. My first question was a fairly obvious one: was he Jersey born and bred? The answer came quickly with a guffaw, 'Absolutely not. I'm from Australia, from Sydney, married to Michele who works for SG Hambros and we moved across to the Island in 2007. I was in banking too and got a transfer to Jersey.' And how had his job at the Town Church come about? 'We began worshipping here and our minister in Sydney knew our Dean and Rector, Bob Key. Bob had been wanting to inaugurate the post of a town centre missioner; the job of verger also came vacant; and the two posts were put together to make the position full-time.'

My next question was obvious too: what were Matthew's twin duties? 'My primary responsibility is for Christian outreach particularly to those working in St Helier; and here my background in banking and finance is relevant. Our major initiative has been Wednesday lunchtime talks: people, whatever their denomination, coming together for a sandwich and the opportunity to share the Gospel with others.' And the job of verger? 'Yes, I wield the dustpan and brush, get my hands dirty, clean the church and the loos and have this terrific frequent opportunity of informally meeting visitors in the church and talking about Jesus and the Christian life.'

Matthew gave a big laugh when I reminded him that Bob Key, assistant minister Tim Neill and himself were all from the evangelical wing of the Church of England. 'Yes, Aussies and South Africans like to hug each other, and the tradition here has perhaps been a little more formal.' I told him that we organists tend to stick close to our consoles and usually manage to avoid all this embracing! The town centre missioner and verger is nonetheless a liberal chap, recognising the

The Town Church

need to cater for everyone, especially non-Christians and newcomers and those with different tastes in musical and worshipping styles.

As a relative newcomer to the Island, living with his wife in the recently renovated and decorated Church House flat, Matthew told me something of his first impressions of Jersey. 'It's a lovely place and, bearing in mind where we come from, you will not be surprised to learn that we are keen sailors. That's our main leisure activity, with racing most weekends. Then there's the stunning beauty of the north coast; so dramatic. I have found the *JEP* essential reading each evening and we are beginning to increase our knowledge of the Island's industries: banking and finance and the interplay with hospitality and tourism. Yes, it's a great place.'

And any last thoughts? Matthew Chase, exuberantly chatting with me in our Town Church pew, brought the conversation back to the worship in this ancient building: 'Exciting things are happening here. We even had kids running around at the main Easter Sunday service. Fantastic.'

~

I walked round the corner from the Town Church into Library Place. I was on my way to meet up with Rod McLoughlin, Jersey's cultural development officer, who has an office on the ground floor of what is one of St Helier's most interesting and historic buildings. The plaque outside tells more:

> This building was given to the Island by
> the Very Reverend Philip Falle
> to house the first public library in Jersey
> 1742-1886

Maurice Boots in his *Architecture in Jersey* presents relevant facts: 'Externally it is a simple building with a plain ashlar granite ground floor surmounted by two brick storeys divided by a plain granite string course'; and Brett reminds us that a successful campaign by conservationists some decades ago saved it from demolition. I walked through the doorway, described by Brett as 'disappointingly modest', and turned left into Rod's office.

Rod McLoughlin's first comments related to our location: 'It's nicely appropriate for the cultural development officer to have his office here. This building may be small and unprepossessing but it is one of the town's most important landmarks that housed what was perhaps the first public library in the British Isles and was saved from demolition as its 1970s neighbours grew up around it.' We continued our conversation on this theme: St Helier, despite unfortunate developments in the last fifty years, having architecture of so much merit from earlier times; how fashionable it was to live in Town in the nineteenth century and how desirable residential streets were created in two or three decades to satisfy demand; how such a trend today would take pressure off Jersey's countryside; how, with dockland developments and the like, many English cities were once again becoming desirable places in which to live.

Falle's Library

It was time to find out more about Rod's background and career. Born in London he came to Jersey when his father, a BBC announcer, retired here in the late 1960s. After Victoria College, he read English at Edinburgh University, applied for a job as a reporter with the *Jersey Evening Post* and in due course became its deputy news editor. 'That gave me a good sense of how the Island works. And I was writing for the paper about cultural matters shortly after the opening of the Arts Centre in 1983. When the post of director became vacant in 1987 I applied – and was appointed to the second job for which I had no obvious qualifications.' (A chuckle from Rod accompanied that last remark.)

Rod served the Arts Centre very successfully for thirteen years: 'There were all sorts of challenges and I was particularly interested in taking the arts to a new audience, examples being festivals, interesting work with the prison and trying to gain the attention and support of those who were not initially predisposed to going to the theatre or to concerts. We also worked up co-operation with the other Channel Islands.'

After the Arts Centre came his five and a half years as chief officer of the Bailiff's Chambers: 'I was perhaps reverting to some of my concerns as a journalist: how the States works; how the Royal Court operates; Jersey's status as a Crown

Dependency; why Jersey is special.' During this time Rod was working for the Bailiff, Sir Philip Bailhache, a leading figure in the setting up of the Arts Centre and someone who has taken a particular interest in the Island's cultural life. And Rod's current role, the States cultural development officer, followed.

Where, I wondered, had the notion of this new position arisen? 'Lots of questions have been asked about the relationship of government with cultural delivery – particularly the arrangements for the funding from government to cultural organisations. There was the feeling that government ought to be doing more than just handing out money and letting recipients get on with it. Culture should also be on government's agenda and taken seriously; government departments need to be brought together so that cultural policy can be co-ordinated. My role is to manage the relationships and get the balance right – to ensure that the structures are in place. At the same time paradoxically there does not need to be too much interference from government and it is also my job to see that cultural organisations are free to get on with it. They need a friend at court and I try to provide that.'

Finally did Rod have any special cultural ambition, a particular gleam in his eye? 'I would love to see a Channel Islands Festival, an arts event taking advantage of the islands' cultural richness: culture felt across the wide spectrum of everyday life. And I believe that such a festival could do this.'

As I left, Rod told me how he had met his wife Julie, formerly a drama teacher at Victoria College. She was directing *A Man for All Seasons* and Rod, *JEP* reporter, was sent to review it. Later, rather pleased with his piece, he rashly asked Julie what she had thought of it. Her reply was this: 'I actually thought that it was rather flippant.' Their friendship, however, developed from there and they lived happily ever after.

~

It was now time for me to head to the Weighbridge and the Esplanade by way of the somewhat dull Conway Street, with a glance left up Bond Street which, says Brett, is 'a good terrace of three-storey houses with most of the Georgian glazing pattern still in place...and well worth a co-ordinated scheme of restoration'. (In three decades there may have been some restoration but little evidence of co-ordination.) At the bottom of Conway Street and on the left is the Southampton Hotel: '1899, a fine cheerfully vulgar example of the seaside architecture of the naughty nineties', says Brett.

At the Weighbridge the fairly recent Liberation statue commands attention. It may not quite be Rodin's *Burghers of Calais*, but it is nonetheless an exciting depiction of the spirit of that memorable day in May 1945. And on the wall nearby there is this announcement:

JOURNEY ROUND St HELIER ~

> On the liberation of Jersey from occupation by German forces on 9 May 1945 British naval officers Sub-lieutenant AD Milln and Surgeon Lieutenant R McDonald draped the Union Jack from a window above this plaque

The wall in question is that of the frontage of what was once the railway station, originally of 1870, and more recently the offices of Jersey Tourism until 2007, now awaiting reincarnation as a restaurant.

Liberation Square

I turned west along the Esplanade and viewed what can only be described as a half-mile of architectural mess. This was once St Helier's seafront with virtually nothing now left of its former coherent terraces of warehouses and hotels. Instead we have a street that lacks all character; for example a recently restored granite façade is squeezed between office developments that reflect the commercial styles of the last thirty or forty years. At one point we come across an office block that

~ THE ROYAL SQUARE TO ELIZABETH CASTLE...

is more French château with mansard roof than anything else; then there are developments using much glass, exciting perhaps but unrelated to neighbouring buildings. The nadir must be a 1970s nine-storey block of flats, Marina Court, which would stick out like a sore finger if there were not others equally damaged nearby.

The eastern end of the Esplanade is now something of a tunnel and on the south side of the road is Jersey's new and very modern bus terminus, Liberation Station, opened by the Lieutenant Governor on 28 September 2007. I entered through its automatic doors and all looked very 'swish' and efficient: information desks, a café, comfortable seating and electronic noticeboards detailing the departure times of the various services. There was no bus to be seen but I caught up with two holidaymakers, Graham and Pauline Cooper from Exeter, who were sitting on a bench, their rucksacks and trekking poles at their feet, waiting for a bus to take them out to Corbière for a day's walking. They told me that they were staying at the new waterfront hotel, the Radisson (on my mental list to visit later on). They had been worried on arrival in the Island since their tourist map stated that it was 'under construction' but were relieved to find the building work finished. I could not resist telling the Coopers that I had written a book, published in 2001, *Hotel West of Albert: Jersey's Waterfront Saga*, describing the campaign with a 7000-signature petition attempting to prevent its construction. I can only say that Mr Cooper's response was somewhat enigmatic: 'Money talks when it comes to planning permission.' What could he have possibly meant? As we chatted (and as I dealt with the Coopers' queries about good restaurants for an evening meal in St Helier) the wall by our bench suddenly swung open to reveal the bus entrance three feet away and ready to take on passengers. The buses are there on the other side of the partitions and hidden from view until the time for embarkation. A very slick operation!

As I left Liberation Station I had a word with Heather Brown behind one of the two information desks. She is employed by Connex, the bus operators, having previously been with their predecessors. She gave the new facility full marks: 'It has pushed Jersey into the modern world. Some of the locals have taken a little time to get familiar with it all; they're shocked by its modernism, more used to waiting in a lay-by or running after the bus.' And she added this final accolade: 'We had a bus driver over on holiday from England and he told us that it beats anything in the UK. The only negative comment came from a local gentleman who came in and told us that he didn't like the colour of the building on the outside – not sunny and happy enough for what was supposed to be a nice island. That's the only 'anti' remark we've had.'

~

JOURNEY ROUND St HELIER ~

I came out of Liberation Station and moved west along to the end of the block. Here a cleverly designed and recent glazed office construction, bordering on the old abattoir buildings, is now the home of Jersey Tourism, and David de Carteret, its director, took me up in the lift and gave me a mug of coffee as we chatted. He started his career with the States in the mid-'70s at Fort Regent as its marketing manager. He then gravitated to the Jersey Conference Bureau before moving into the mainstream tourism operation in the mid-1980s. He was quick to tell me what had changed: in those days 25,000 visitor beds and now a figure more like 12,000. But he quickly emphasised that the quality was now so much higher than previously.

Tourism

I wanted to learn more about the current tourism situation but first asked David about his actual responsibilities. 'My job is about marketing Jersey as a tourism destination: leisure tourism, business tourism and for conferences. And we have a broader role too such as the marketing of Jersey Royal potatoes.' I also wished to know about the financing of Tourism and David told me that the cost was £6½m but that the contribution to Jersey's economy was something in the order of £230m. 'It is still a drop in the ocean compared with what the finance industry contributes, but it is still important economically. And remember what tourism does to our quality of life as local residents. Many of the amenities that we enjoy in our leisure time might not exist if it were not for the visitor spend within the Island.'

David reminded me about the boom years of the 1960s and '70s: how in those days British Rail staff on free boat tickets boosted the industry and, along with *Bergerac* and all that, Jersey was a mass-market destination. 'Since then the market has changed significantly: people come for a shorter stay; they're looking for more quality things to do, for good food and for three-star-plus accommodation whereas two-star was the main choice in former years. And we're working hard to open up the European market; and low-cost travel, with new flights starting all the time, is of great importance.'

What were David de Carteret's hopes for the future? 'We must keep Jersey as reasonable value for money, keeping our costs competitive. We have a good and improving range of accommodation and our natural environment is superb. It is about having this experience delivered in a way that is acceptable to our customers. And an important point is this: Jersey is a destination where people live as opposed to its being just a constructed holiday resort. When people visit they are participating in a living environment; they are joining a community and hopefully having that very engaging experience.'

David brought me down to the ground floor and said his farewells. As I was leaving I noticed behind the reception desk and giving polished, professional service to visitors was someone I knew from a few years back. Maria da Silva, Miss Battle in 2002, had kindly allowed me to interview her for my *Speaking of Jersey*, published in 2003. Jersey-born and educated and of Portuguese parents, she has worked at Tourism since 1999 and it was very good to meet her again, this time in her working environment. Having finished with her customers, she was able to talk to me for a few minutes: over the years things had moved on, with promotion to supervisor and then to assistant manager and she was now no longer living in St Ouen but able to walk to work from her St Helier home. Some years ago she had told me of her big decision to dedicate her life to Jersey and not Madeira. Was she still firm in that idea? 'Absolutely. I have now been with Tourism for eight years and am very passionate about the Island and my work.' Was she, I asked, still a great ambassador for Jersey? 'Thank you very much for saying that. I would like to think so.' As Maria turned back to help her enquiring visitors, I had few doubts as to her great value in so strongly and engagingly promoting the Island.

~

I emerged from Tourism; it was time for another cup of coffee. Crossing the road I headed for the arched opening opposite. This is the entrance to Anley Street and on the left under the arch is a door with carpeted stairs on the other side leading up to The Green Olive, a small but busy restaurant presided over by Paul Le Brocq. He is a Jerseyman (could this be in doubt concerning someone bearing that particular surname?) who started aged sixteen cooking at Longueville Manor. Then followed periods in the kitchens of the Grand and other famous Island hotels, a spell in the United States and, back in Jersey, running a beach café. A brief period selling motor cars preceded purchase of The Green Olive in 2002.

It is a restaurant with a special appeal and flavour: 'We don't do any red meat whatsoever; yes to fresh fish, chicken and vegetarian dishes and, as members of Genuine Jersey, we always use local produce as much as possible.' I then asked Paul what were the main problems of running a Jersey restaurant. His answer came without too much hesitation: 'It's the Regulations and Undertakings legislation which limits who I employ. R and U tell me that I have to engage equal numbers of locals and non-locals; it is very hard. And then there are the costs – everything more expensive here than in the UK – while at the same time we must keep our pricing competitive. The new GST doesn't help.'

Paul was keen to tell me about his establishment's good reputation: outright winner of the Menu du Terroir competition promoting Jersey produce in 2005 and runner-up in 2007. (The certificates were on the wall to prove his success.) That good name serves him well: 'We get a fair number of tourists – spin-off from the Grand, the Revere and the Pomme d'Or for instance; people in their reception areas know of us. We've also had guests staying at Longueville Manor coming to eat here.' 'And the future of tourism?' I asked. 'My mum and dad had a guesthouse for twenty years and they sold out at the right time. Agriculture has pretty well disappeared too, and the Island is geared up to the finance sector above all else. But I am not complaining: many of my lunchtime clients are business people and I value their custom.'

The Green Olive, certainly at lunchtime, is somewhat weather-dependent: 'If it is sunny, people eat their sandwiches outside; if it is cloudy, then I am very busy.' By now I had finished my coffee and the chefs and waitress were busy getting ready for the lunchtime service. As I took my leave, was Paul just a little apprehensive about what I would write following our chat? I told him not to worry and said that I would expect a meal on the house if my piece boosted the custom of his already popular and distinctive St Helier eating-place.

~ THE ROYAL SQUARE TO ELIZABETH CASTLE...

~

It was time for me to give my attention to the Waterfront, the history of which, from the 1979 decision of the States to in-fill this bit of sea to the failed campaign in the year 2000 to 'stop the hotel', I had recounted in my *Hotel West of Albert* published in 2001. I crossed the Esplanade, circled the roundabout and headed south down the Route du Port Elizabeth and made for Maritime House. This handsome modern building dates from 1999 and for several years was a prominent feature in an otherwise undeveloped area. Its interesting design is now hidden as flats and warehouses have surrounded and removed it from view. Maritime House is the headquarters of Jersey's Customs and Immigration Service and also of its Harbours Department and I dropped in to chat with both the Director, Immigration and Nationality, John Noel, and, upstairs, the Harbourmaster, Captain Howard Le Cornu.

John first told me that the Noels were originally all from St Martin's, and indeed he went to its primary school before going on to Victoria College and then joining the Civil Service immediately from school. 'I came straight into what was then called the Aliens' Office and I have been here ever since.' John is one of the three directors in the Customs and Immigration Service, with immigration being his particular responsibility. He sketched for me an interesting history: 'Over the years there was always a move to integrate Customs and Immigration, and we had a combined force in the 1970s and 1980s called the Port Officers. The departments then separated again, but we have come full circle and now have a frontier section combining the duties of immigration officers and customs preventive officers.'

I asked John what were Jersey's main immigration problems. He was quick to tell me that there are not the UK difficulties: 'We don't have the problem of asylum seekers. A lot of people, including some of our politicians, fail to grasp the fact that the States of Jersey have very little control over immigration from abroad. As far as immigration goes we are effectively a UK port and part of the common travel area which includes the UK, the Channel Islands, the Isle of Man and the Republic of Ireland. It follows that in immigration matters I am responsible to the Lieutenant Governor and not to our Home Affairs Minister. And concerning deportation affairs I deal with His Excellency and not the States. What, I asked John Noel, was to stop me landing illegally from abroad in a small boat at, say, Grève de Lecq? He replied, 'It's a problem for the whole of the UK, but we have very few such cases. There's not a lot going for economic migrants in Jersey; we don't have the same social benefits; there are no large ethnic communities into which they could disappear; and we have law-abiding employers who would be unwilling to give jobs to illegal immigrants.'

I wanted to know something too of the customs side of the service, although not John's main responsibility. 'Customs have two main functions: the collection of revenue and also the enforcement side – control of drugs but also anything that crosses the borders illegally such as animals or, for example, ivory. Some years ago the police formed a special branch and we have a good relationship with them at the frontiers.'

Finally John Noel, in his very modern Maritime House office and a few months from retirement after over forty years' service, told me of future plans: 'My biggest pastime at the moment is family history. I'm just coming to the end of my three years as President of the Family History Society. So there's a lot of work to be done on the history of the Noel family; I've traced our line in St Martin back to the early 1700s. And I am already under orders to serve as a volunteer at Jersey Archive, giving help and advice to those investigating their genealogy. All this will keep me happily occupied.'

~

I left John Noel and climbed to the first floor of Maritime House to see Captain Howard Le Cornu. He actually wears two hats, having been appointed Harbourmaster in 2002 and Chief Executive of Jersey Harbours three years later. From the age of thirteen he had wanted to go to sea and, after taking his O-levels at Hautlieu, joined the Blue Star Line and spent the next twelve years sailing round the world. In due course as a chief officer he transferred to the ferries – to Channel Island Ferries where he became Master of that favourite ship, Corbière; 'a superb job,' he explained, 'as its ship's captain with much pilotage experience coming in and out of local waters.' Then followed a period with the cross-Solent ferries, an MBA studied at Southampton University, a post as development director with Red Funnel for new high-speed services and then eventually his present appointment back home in Jersey.

What, I wanted to know, was the range of his current responsibilities? 'Overall I am accountable for the operation of the harbours and the territorial waters of the Island. Safety, policing, financial control all come into it. There are three distinct areas: the freight ports (without which Jersey would not survive); the Jersey coastguards, rebranded recently as the search and rescue blue light authority; and marine leisure. For all this I have about 70 staff rising to 120 in the season.'

Then came what was for me something of a bombshell: I asked Captain Le Cornu about developments in the future, and this was his response: 'On the table we have plans for a new port altogether – new marinas and a new commercial port to the east of Albert where the current reclamation site now is.' The Harbourmaster continued: 'Ro-ro has grown exponentially over the last thirty years; we are stretched at the seams in the Elizabeth Terminal complex. Our new developments will give us more room for warehousing, transferring the ro-ro berths over there and separating the dirtier commercial activities from marine leisure and housing west of Albert. And we also have a plan for a cruise liner berth, and that would be a considerable and exciting contribution in so many ways to the Island.'

And the timing for all this and its funding? 'Over the next ten years hopefully, and these new port developments would be financed by the revenues gained from the current space which would be released for domestic and leisure development.' There is no doubting Captain Le Cornu's enthusiasm for and confidence in his plans: 'They ensure the port's viability both in terms of expanded space and on a sound financial footing, undoubtedly for generations to come.'

I came away excited myself: perhaps one day a sequel to *Hotel West of Albert*. And its title? Surely *Port East of Albert*.

~

From Maritime House I wandered along to the seemingly doomed Elizabeth Terminal. The inscription outside reads as follows:

> Elizabeth Harbour
> This harbour was opened by
> Her Majesty the Queen
> Thursday 25th May 1989

Little did Her Majesty realise the potentially ephemeral nature of this not very becoming structure, already within two decades rather faded and shabby.

At the door stood a smart and authoritative young man wearing a luminous yellow jacket bearing on its left breast the words, 'Jersey Harbours Port Operations'. Here was one of Captain Le Cornu's staff, by name Stuart Johnson. Stuart told me what his job was: 'It's not easy to sum up in a few words. We do lots of different things around the harbour: making sure that the operation runs smoothly, looking after the security side and the parking. When there's a boat in, it is our job to ensure that passengers disembark and embark safely. We keep an eye on everything that's happening.'

Was Stuart, I asked, a Jerseyman? 'No; I've been over here seven years. I come from Cornwall actually. My girlfriend got a job in the Island and I followed her. I started with Condor Ferries and then came over to the Harbours.' And how did life in Jersey compare with that in Cornwall? 'Oh, a lot better. I think Jersey's a fabulous place. The housing's expensive; that's the only thing. But I've never regretted the move. We live in St Helier close to work, and I can cycle in.' Was Stuart a contented fellow? 'Definitely yes,' was the prompt reply.

I now moved through the automatic doors into the drab terminal itself. Seated on a bench and waiting with various generations of his family for the ferry to St Malo was Frenchman Marc Tollamare from Fontainebleau. I had approached the right man; his English was perfect. They had all been staying in Jersey for a couple of days and this had been their first visit. 'We have really enjoyed it. The weather has been perfect and we have been round the Island and visited all the small bays. And the Monterey Hotel has looked after us well.' Here then was another contented stranger.

Would I strike lucky a third time? I approached the HD Ferries desk and, after a little persuading, Sonia Rodrigues, working as a booking clerk, was willing to answer my questions as I held my recording machine over the counter. Sonia told me that she was born in Venezuela and had come to Jersey four years previously to join her Portuguese parents who lived here. What did she like about the Island? 'It is a quiet place to live. We have a flat in Town, comfortable but it could be cheaper? Jersey is nice.'

Stuart, Marc and Sonia had all given Jersey a vote of confidence. I did not suggest that for a different point of view they should read the letters page of the *Jersey Evening Post* or tune in to the BBC Radio Jersey phone-in.

~

I now came back from Elizabeth Terminal up the Route du Port Elizabeth towards the bleak cluster of buildings, hardly architecturally distinguished, that houses the Aquasplash swimming pool and Cineworld, Jersey's multi-screen facility. (Might we just as well have been in Milton Keynes or Dagenham?) I was once given some hope by a local architect/town planner: he told me that such developments do not have to last for ever, and that the value of the land on which these particular buildings stand could allow for their demolition and replacement rather sooner than one might expect.

I wandered in to Aquasplash and at the reception desk encountered the duty manager, Adrian de St George. After school at Les Quennevais he had done an advanced vocation certificate in leisure and recreation at Highlands College and then became a lifeguard, having become full-time here in 2004. Through the glass walls he pointed out for me the amenity's salient features: 'Here's the main pool, with its moveable floor and boom to separate the diving area, and that's the leisure pool with its wave machine and three flumes. No, we're not a States concern; it's a company called Serco that runs Aquasplash for the States.' I learned more: the place is open from a surprisingly early 6.30 a.m. until 8 p.m; there are swimming lessons, private party hire arrangements, a part of the leisure pool outside with something called a 'lazy river', and also saunas and steam rooms. I have to say that I was not tempted to try out any of the facilities, thanked Adrian and moved on next door to the cinema.

Now I do sometimes make use of Cineworld, whatever my opinion of the building's outside appearance; for me there are few things nicer than a good film at five o'clock, a fairly empty auditorium (with less noise from the other customers, the popcorn and the food wrappings) and an extremely comfortable cinema seat. Both the operations manager, Shaun McKernan, and the general manager, Elaine Rabet, were kind enough to talk to me and led me up to the first floor café area. Shaun is from Weymouth and has been at Cineworld for three years. Elaine is Scots and has been in charge since the cinema opened in 2002. I learned from them something of the day-to-day operation: no problems with staff recruitment; the busiest times being the weekends; just two technicians needed to operate the ten screens. I wondered whether they had any discretion about the films shown and sensed that they screened what headquarters sent them. Why, I asked, was one screen not reserved for art house films? Elaine gave me the answer: 'It is a question of logistics. There are only a certain number of prints and here in Jersey we are not just down the motorway.' And Shaun added this concerning choice of films: 'Yes, we do put in requests but…,' and his answer tailed off at this point. I also mentioned to them that Cineworld was not the most admired architectural structure in the Island. Shaun replied laconically, 'Yes, I have heard that said.' Both Shaun and Elaine like living in Jersey but neither seems what could be termed a film buff. This was Elaine's answer to that query: 'Yes I am, but I used to see more films before I came to work here.'

Our conversation over, I thanked Shaun and Elaine for sparing me their time and they then took me along to see the VIP boxes which two of the ten screens possess, with particularly comfortable and select seating behind a glass wall and waiter service for refreshments. I also saw something of the projectors and sound equipment and found out, my curiosity about Cineworld finally satisfied, that the films are still shown from reels and that the expected digital revolution is still a few years off.

~

It was now time for me to head towards the Radisson SAS Waterfront Hotel, the building 'west of Albert' that rose despite the campaign of 1999/2000 – with public meetings, much press coverage and a petition that attracted over 9000 signatures – which attempted to prevent its construction. As I walked towards it I was passing hoardings surrounding a huge building site and carrying the message, 'Castle Quay'. Then I came upon what could be termed a large pavilion. This turned out to be the marketing suite of Dandara, the company responsible for the development of Castle Quay and much else both in Jersey, the Isle of Man and Britain. The person who could tell me more about both Castle Quay and Dandara was Christine Holmes, a consultant responsible for the firm's marketing and PR and, in her words, 'very much part of the Dandara team and one who cares passionately for the company and what we achieve.'

Christine first of all gave me an account of their waterfront development: planning permission granted and designed by Eric Kuhne (the architect responsible for Darling Harbour in Sydney and the Miami waterfront), with 147 one- two- and three-bedroom apartments in the first phase, and commercial space for restaurants, café-bars, chic boutique retail and the like. The original scheme had contained the three controversial towers which, after public consultation, were now no longer included. (Christine handed me a copy of the original brochure and I now began to wonder – was this heresy? - whether the towers might actually have enhanced the development.)

I also quizzed Christine about Dandara itself. She told me this: 'The company started in 1988 in the Isle of Man and has grown exponentially since. We have been in Jersey since 1996 and to date have built 640 units of accommodation in the Island. The West Park Apartments and Chateau Royale at Grouville are also Dandara developments. And we are doing much city centre work in Glasgow, Manchester, Birmingham and London. We're a big organisation, employing 350 people here in Jersey.'

I then plucked up courage and said to Christine Holmes that Dandara seemed to attract much hostile comment from some in the Island who were suggesting that the company was taking Jersey over. Christine's reply was firm and confident: 'Have you actually been inside any of our developments to see the quality of what we are providing? Also, don't be under the misapprehension that, if we were not here, then the buildings for which we are responsible would not be happening; another developer would be involved instead. And remember: we who work for Dandara are not shipped in during the day and shipped out at night; we live here; this is our island too and we love and cherish it as well. Yes, likes and dislikes of architecture are a subjective matter. Take West Park; there was much affection for the Pav but it had been empty for 12 years and derelict, with the cliff behind falling into what was left of the building. We actually paid £1m for the cliff to be stabilised before we could start building the apartments.'

We returned to the matter of Castle Quay, with the first phase due to be completed in 2011 and the second phase with another 195 apartments by mid-2012. 'It is a significant investment for us, and that is relevant and overlooked by those people who criticise Dandara. Here we are, a locally registered company paying local taxes and putting our money back into Jersey's economy. That is the point missed time and time again by our critics.'

Christine Holmes has been in Jersey for over 12 years and is unhesitating in her love for the Island. 'I guess that it is one of those places where you go away on holiday, have a fantastic time, but then come back and just go "wow" and consider how lucky one is to be coming home. With our beaches, our countryside, our restaurants, our safe environment, we have a great quality of life and are fortunate to have the opportunity of living in Jersey.'

~ *THE ROYAL SQUARE TO ELIZABETH CASTLE...*

~

I walked into the Radisson's capacious reception hall with its huge aquarium, not wanted by its previous owners, ITV, and gifted to the hotel (apparently the grateful recipients had to meet the cost of transport and installation which came to £85,000). Ted Clucas met me there and took me through the restaurant to a quiet spot where we chatted and had a coffee. Ted, a Jersey resident since 1972, is chairman of Herald Trust (and was President of Jersey's Association of Trust Companies for four years in the late 1990s). He is also chairman of Jersey Waterfront Hotel Holding Ltd, and it is that company which financed and owns this new and large addition to the Island's hotel scene. Radisson SAS (the letters stand for Scandinavian Airline Systems) manage the establishment on behalf of Hotel Holding with a contract for 25 years and an option for a further 20.

I started with a direct question for Ted Clucas: what did he say to the criticisms levelled by some at the hotel's appearance and its siting? His response was clear: 'I think that whatever you do in a small community, you are not going to please all the people all the time. Also this location is land created out of nothing; suddenly a 200-bedroom hotel appears in the middle of nowhere and that comes as a shock to many. At present it sticks out prominently; in six to seven years' time when it is surrounded with all the other developments, you won't notice it at all.'

Ted then told me of Radisson's enthusiasm in taking over its management: 'It took us twelve weeks to negotiate the deal from start to finish. The CEO from Brussels actually signed the piece of paper in a taxi on his way back to the airport. Radisson have more than 400 hotels throughout the world and reckon that this has the best views of them all. They also have a fairly phlegmatic executive chef of the whole group; he came over and told us that our kitchens were better than any others. So, you see, we seem to have done one or two things right.'

I then learned something of the hotel's prefabricated construction, carried out by local contractors, Camerons Ltd. Ted told me that, considering the size and complexity of the development, it had all gone very smoothly. 'Do you know how much the hotel weighs?' he asked me. He also provided the answer: '13,000 tons, all transported over in 14 weeks. It was the biggest freight contract that Condor has ever had.' And the clientele targeted? ' Primarily it is a four-star business hotel, but of course we very much have an eye for the tourist side as well. And what we can offer the locals is also of great importance. Thus this new hotel opens a whole new market as well as a different sector of the existing one. And Radisson have their own considerable marketing machine; they can generate the business through that and not have to rely solely on local promotion. No other hospitality organisation in the Island can make that boast, we being the only internationally branded hotel in Jersey. And bear this in mind: my business partner and I went into this when, quite frankly, there were probably better and more profitable investments for our resources, but we considered that the Island needed what has been provided here.'

I was about to thank Ted Clucas and take my leave when he told me that he would show me the hotel's *pièce de résistance*. He took me up in the lift to the fifth floor, and through double doors we entered a massive boardroom with its 180° of glass from floor to high ceiling and stunning views of Elizabeth Castle and out over St Aubin's Bay to the open sea. It was a climactic conclusion to an absorbing encounter.

~

I walked away from the hotel, heading once more for the Esplanade, this time its western extremity. In front of me was the 'upturned boat' café, La Frégate. This building, perhaps more appropriate for Disneyworld than here, was a 1997 construction and at the time the pride and joy, along with the Steam Clock, of the body charged with the developments west of Albert, the Waterfront Enterprise Board. I popped in to the café, ordered a cappuccino and had a chat over the counter with Deborah Caeres, in charge of the till. I discovered that Deborah, from Madeira, had only been in Jersey for three weeks. 'My husband has been here for three months,' she told me, 'working here as a kitchen porter, and our child, one and a half years old, is coming in a fortnight's time.' I complimented Deborah on her excellent English and she replied, 'People tell me that I have a good accent. Thank you.' Her first impressions of Jersey seemed to be favourable; she and her husband were living in a St Helier guesthouse and hoping one day for an apartment. And as to La Frégate? 'I like it – inside I like better than the outside. The owner has told me that, when it was designed, it wasn't meant to be an upside-down boat. It just turned out that way.' On that dubious note I finished my coffee, wished Deborah well and took my leave.

~

Having made it through the traffic across the busy Esplanade, I moved a hundred yards up Kensington Place to meet someone I know well in my capacity as an organist who plays regularly for funerals. Andy Errington-Rennell is a co-director of undertakers Pitcher and Le Quesne and began by telling me something of his early life: 'I was brought up in St Mary but was a town boy after my grandfather got rid of the farm. I started my working life as a coxswain on the harbour pilots' cutter. Then came 1983: I'd become involved with the St Catherine's inshore lifeboat, had an accident when we were hit by a large wave, cracked my spine and it was 18 months before my back recovered. And that was the end of my boating career.' Retail security work with Voisins and employment with Securicor followed, prior to his joining Pitcher and Le Quesne in 1989.

I asked Andy how he had started as a funeral director. 'I came straight in on the public side, learning how to arrange funerals, familiarising myself with the various laws dealing with burial, cremation, exhumation and burial at sea. Then I studied the basics of probate so that I could offer advice when called upon. And I mastered the names of all the Island's religious ministers, the organists, the registrars, the doctors and most of the lawyers.'

What was it like coming across people at an emotional, distressing time for them? Andy answered me in this way: 'It is something that comes with experience. I think that you have got to be a patient person. Sometimes you have to be a shoulder to cry on; equally you have got to be prepared for some of those grieving to shout and bawl their heads off at you. With bereaved people you just can't tell what state they will be in. Sometimes I go into a house and they are laughing and joking – their way of coping; on other occasions and in different households everybody can be deeply distressed and crying. And you have to have the compassion to be able to give somebody a hug; nowadays one is not supposed to, but I'm of the old school and still do.'

I learned more about the business: the 24-hour on-call system; the permanent team of pall-bearers who are also taxi-drivers; the in-house staff that includes the person qualified to carry out embalming when the option of 'hygienic treatment' is taken up. Also Andy told me that under Jersey law it is funeral directors who supervise exhumations, with him having carried out the highest number in the Island, including the 27 bodies that had to be moved from the All Saints cemetery in the Parade when it was re-ordered.

Our conversation ended with Andy telling me about burials at sea. 'Not many places in the British Isles have the licence for this; Jersey is fairly unique, perhaps because we are an island of mariners. I have improved the way we carry these out. We use the *Duke of Normandy* States tug. Environmental issues come into it and there are no coffins. Brand-new galvanised chain, twice the weight of the deceased, is attached to the board on which the deceased, with three layers of calico wrapping, is laid. We sail out to the burial ground which is roughly three and a half miles south-west of St Helier harbour and just the other side of a deep shelf in the seabed.'

Before I left, Andy took me to the back of Pitcher and Le Quesne's Kensington Place premises and showed me the unoccupied one of their three tasteful chapels of rest. I passed the door to the mortuary but did not enter and, on leaving, thanked Andy for telling me about a profession that is both an essential service to the community and one requiring both skill and compassion.

~

I returned to the Esplanade and turned left, passing the Grand Hotel. Was it feeling just a little peeved, with its new neighbour having recently risen in stark if uncongenial modernity in front of it and on the waterfront? The Grand can give the Radisson more than 100 years, having been built in 1890 and, despite alterations and additions since, still retaining what Maurice Boots describes as 'its five great gables giving the façade a feeling of breadth'. I was actually heading for the new West Park Apartments and, in particular, the flat of Angela Trigg. I rang the security buzzer, was admitted and took the very swish lift up to the first floor where Angela, door open, was waiting for me. I entered a huge room – sitting room, dining room and kitchen all in one – with what can only be termed fabulous views across to Elizabeth Castle and the sea.

I first wanted to know more about Angela, born in St Brelade, educated from the age of fifteen in Spain and then a linguist and interpreter, studying German, Spanish, Dutch and, later in life, Japanese. 'I married a Dutchman and we lived in Switzerland for 16 years and had two daughters. Sadly the marriage failed and I carried on with languages: wonderful jobs in the diplomatic service and with the Ministry of Defence.' She and her second husband, Rob, returned to Jersey in 1981 where she continued with her interpreting and her work with the police. Much involvement with youth organisations, especially after the death of her second daughter in 1989, and crime prevention made her a most suitable member of the Board of Visitors at Greenfields, the Island's secure unit for youth. Rob sadly died suddenly just after their move into West Park Apartments in 2007. She continues to pursue her varied interests, especially the twinning and reconciliation events with Germany and her annual pilgrimage taking former Jersey deportees back to where they were interned for two and a half years in southern Germany.

Angela Trigg and I were sitting chatting in this stunning pastiche Art Deco building, designed by local architects Naish Waddington, on the site of the much loved Pav – later known as Inn on the Park – over which there had been a ferocious and unsuccessful fight by admirers to save it from demolition. How did it feel to live where once there had been a building held in affection by so many? Angela's response was extremely interesting and a surprise: 'I loved the Pav. I grew up in that generation when little girls used to have their parties there. There was this magnificent, beautifully sprung dance floor. And not only that, my father, Douglas Tanguy, now eighty-nine and still playing the piano in the evenings at the St Brelade's Bay Hotel, had a big band which he led. Most people will remember him at the old Woodville Hotel, but there were the traditional jazz nights at the Pav and all those other big occasions when my father and his band performed there.'

This for Angela is a remarkable link: the old Pav, where she partied and her father made music, and her new home in this handsome building with its sophisticated Modernist lines and commanding position above the sea. 'This place has so many memories for me from childhood. I can sit here, mull things over and be inspired. You can never tire of the view; each day is different, and it was rather scary in the recent storms with the water at high tide breaking across the road. And don't forget: the Battle of Flowers and the Battle of Britain display – just outside my windows!'

~

Elizabeth Castle, the end of my second walk, was in reach. The tide was on its way out; I eschewed the amphibian ferry, Charming Nancy (no kittling of my fancy there), and set out across the causeway, at one point having to wade through six inches of retreating water. In front of me was what Boots describes as 'the silhouette of a great modern battleship at anchor', and there can be no doubting that this iconic and aesthetically satisfying complex of military buildings is, again in Boots's words, 'the most complete and finest example of its kind in the British Isles'. Brett also waxes eloquent: 'Elizabeth Castle – 16th century and later; on a highly dramatic site, some 1000 yards from the seawall at West Park and accessible on foot only between tides, a highly romantic range of fortifications'. This is an islet 500 yards long. From the sixth to the ninth century it was a monastic settlement; the castle was built between 1600 and 1750; the handsome eight-bay Governor's House was completed in time to be occupied by Sir Walter Raleigh, sworn in as Governor in September 1600, later being the home for the future Charles II in 1646 as Prince of Wales and also from 1649 to 1650 during the Civil War. Then there are the fine 18th century barrack buildings surrounding the impressive sandy parade ground. Far later, during the Occupation, the Germans added their bit as well, and the remains of their bunkers and strong-points have been carefully preserved. It was with a sense of understandable thrill that I checked in at the entrance gate and made my way into the heart of this fine military complex to be greeted by Jon Troy, the Castle's gardien since the summer of 2006.

Jon and I sat down on a bench at the side of the parade ground and he told me something about himself: 'Yes, I am from the family of George Troy and Sons, Master Stevedores; George was my grandfather. After leaving Hautlieu I went to Highlands College and did a two-year hotel management course. Then I became a chef, working in Switzerland, on the QE2 for a short spell and in some of Jersey's à la carte restaurants. But with the unsocial hours it's a young man's profession; I saw the light, applied to the Heritage Trust as a site guide and worked at Mont Orgueil. I have always been interested in history, loved coming to Elizabeth Castle as a youngster and relished the opportunity of taking up the job here when the post fell vacant in 2006.'

And the gardien's duties? 'They are multi-faceted really. I'm responsible for the security of the Castle, looking after health and safety issues and the landscape and managing the gardeners. Basically it is the day-to-day management of what is an important historic and tourist attraction and all that that entails.' And any snags in living here throughout the year? 'It is a matter of planning in advance as to how and when my partner and I get to and from the mainland. A four-wheel drive vehicle is essential, and we buy them second-hand; the salt would not be kind to a new car.'

Elizabeth Castle

I wondered whether the Heritage Trust had a vision for the future of Elizabeth Castle. Jon replied, 'Like Mont Orgueil the possibilities are big; there are many spaces here that are not used. It's all about money but there is much that could be done.' Jon also said that more holiday lets could not be ruled out nor the updating of displays. But he did emphasise the contribution of the volunteers who, besides other duties, fire the signal gun every day and organise the noonday parade – 'it's fantastic fun for all.'

I asked Jon whether he had an opinion on the relative proximity of the waterfront developments and, in particular, the Radisson Hotel. His reply gave me pause for thought: 'Looking shoreward from here at the waterfront expansion, you see how quickly the town is encroaching. Being a Jerseyman I remember when the nearest point of land was once the corner of the old abattoir building; not any longer. It worries me; it's almost as though the Castle is being swept away on a tide of development.'

Despite that, Jon Troy is a contented man: 'My job here is a dream come true.

~ THE ROYAL SQUARE TO ELIZABETH CASTLE...

In my spare time I grow vegetables, and where better to do my fishing – off the breakwater or the storm beach.'

~

It was a fine afternoon and I struck out along the Castle breakwater, built in the later 1800s as part of an ambitious and partially unrealised scheme to enlarge the harbour. Halfway to the end and perched on a rocky outcrop, is a 12th century oratory, being all that remains of the early monastic settlement here and on the site of the martyrdom of St Helier in the sixth century at the hands of pirates (so it is said). No visit to Elizabeth Castle is surely complete without visiting, in Brett's words, 'this extremely attractive stone building of extreme simplicity...reached by a curling flight of stone steps...A natural cavity in the rock is reputed to have been the saint's bed'. I followed Brett's instructions, then walked to the end of the breakwater and turned for home.

As I came back towards the Castle I bumped into two tourists, Englishman Ian Hughes and his Australian wife Kathleen. Chatting with them, I discovered that they had only arrived in Jersey that morning on their first visit. 'We've just had a wonderful lunch at the Bistro Central, looked after very well by Michel,' Ian told me. 'We're staying at a boutique hotel behind the Grand and, no, we didn't take the transport and instead walked across the causeway.' And what were their thoughts on the Castle? 'It's fascinating, with so much history and heritage; St Helier and Sir Walter Raleigh and all that.' Ian and Kathleen were only here for four days. I suggested that they also worked Mont Orgueil into their holiday schedule.

I climbed the wooden stair from the breakwater and was passing through the Castle parade ground when I encountered Gunner Coom – or at least David Coom doing duty that afternoon in his 1781 uniform: tricorn hat, breeches, buckle shoes, with flintlock musket on his right, bayonet on the left and, in front, the pouch for his cartridges. He told me what he was about: 'I am walking round and talking to visitors. We have one permanent chap who does this and I am standing in for him this week. The public get sucked in to the parade before noon each day – on the square here. We march the men to the cannon, and the ladies come along behind as, I suppose, camp followers. Then volunteers go down into the gun pit with the gunner, and the cannon is eventually fired.' Beside us there was a lady listening in to our conversation. She butted in at this point: 'The gun makes an extremely loud noise.'

It was opportune for me to have encountered this little bit of historical colour which provides a nice aid for Elizabeth Castle's many visitors. I made towards the Castle entrance and, once again giving Charming Nancy the cold shoulder, stepped out along the now dry causeway for the shore at West Park.

2

The Royal Square and up Rouge Bouillon by way of King Street and The Parade

Before leaving the Royal Square for my second stroll round Town, I thought that I would have a chat with a few of those using its plentiful benches while contemplating the quiet and traffic-free scene. First I was thwarted in my approaches by a lady munching a sandwich who told me briskly that she was both busy and stressed before being collected by her male partner and removed to the other side of the square. Then across the concourse came the familiar figure of a Jurat whom I have known for 35 years. Surely he would oblige. Sadly, no; he also was far too busy and heading for important duties in the adjacent Royal Court. As it turned out, he sat down and we chatted animatedly for at least ten minutes (if only I had had the Dictaphone running!) with his final parting sally being that, if I persisted in waylaying strangers here, I was making myself liable for arrest. I tried once more, moving across to the seats under the Union Club's façade and having a chat with a middle-aged man called Andy who was devouring a roll and drinking from a paper mug of coffee purchased nearby at the café (the former public lavatories) at the top of Broad Street. Andy told me that he came to Jersey 19 years before from Wales. A carpenter by trade, this was his day off and he was taking it easy in what he described as 'this nice relaxing place'. Did he like Jersey, I asked. 'I'm happy here and have no intention of leaving the Island. I have my housing qualifications and bought a flat three years ago.' I asked Andy whether he knew whose was the gilded statue in front of us. 'No'; with George II he was not acquainted. And Jersey history? 'I don't know much about it, but there were various wars and the French kept trying to come across.' What had brought him to Jersey? 'A chap in my pub at home had been here and recommended it for a change of scene and I've stayed ever since.' My last question was, I thought, appropriate for this place at the heart of the Island's government. I asked Andy whether he followed the Island's politics. I suspect that his answer would have been that of many similar inhabitants from elsewhere: 'No. I've never registered and never actually voted.'

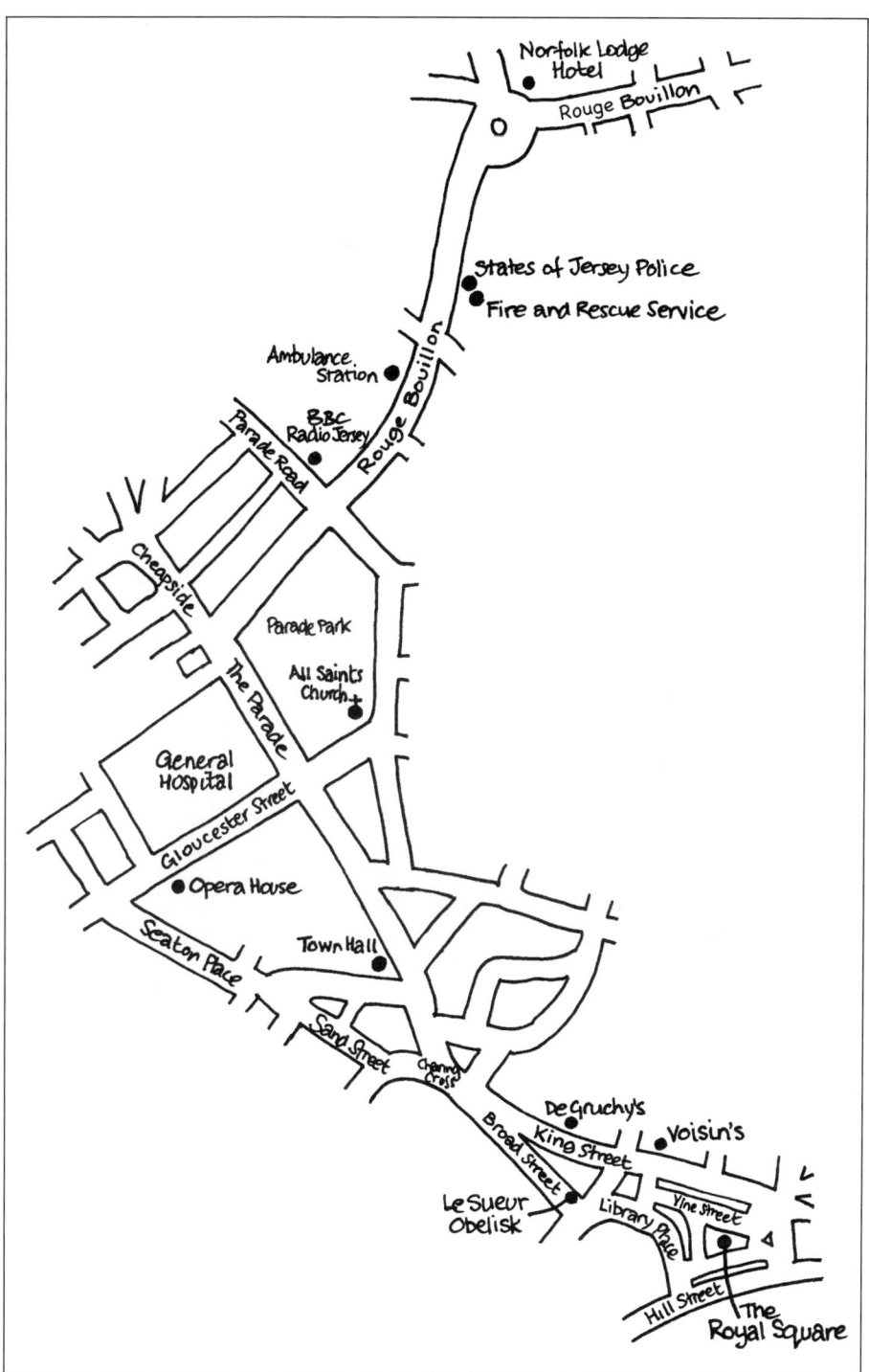

JOURNEY ROUND St HELIER ~

Saddened as a student of politics by Andy's all too typical apathy, I made my farewells and moved on to the top of Broad Street and its impressive Le Sueur Obelisk. Brett is anxious to point out that this memorial to Pierre Le Sueur, 1811-1853 and five times Connétable of St Helier, is not a monolith. The monument's lions' masks were originally water fountains for the horses at the adjacent cab stand (the taxis were moved away only two or three years ago) and this pleasing pile is nicely sited in alignment with Library Place so that George II and it are visible from each other.

Le Sueur Obelisk, Broad Street

I now slipped through Brook Street to the Rue de Derrière (no sniggering at the back of the class please), better known as King Street, admiring on the corner the nicely preserved and extensive 1830s shop front of CT Maine, the Jewellers, with its pretty frilly cast-iron railing above the fascia, and popped in to Voisins Department Store, anxious to have a word with its managing director, Gerald

Voisin, successor to his great-great-great-grandfather who founded his draper's business on this very site in 1837.

Gerald welcomed me to his office at the top of the store and told me about himself: born in 1963 and educated at Victoria College Prep and then at Blundell's School in Devon. He did not fancy going to university and came back to the family business, learning it, with a short spell working at Harrods, from the roots up. I asked Gerald to confirm that his was now the only big retail outlet in the Island that was still Jersey-owned. 'Yes; the others are now all UK companies. There were once six or so department stores in St Helier; now there are just ourselves and de Gruchy's. You see, department stores are challenging; they soak up money as one constantly improves the facilities for the customer who is ever-demanding these days. Retail is highly competitive; we have seen ten years of deflation in the products we sell – 40% deflation in the price of our goods and at the same time 40% inflation in terms of staff costs and fuel, etc. Our rates doubled a few years back. It's not easy even if, like us, we own the property. Here we are, sitting on this £20m asset and necessarily wondering what else we could do with it. And another problem is this: most of the young in Jersey go into the finance industry and few of them into retail. We now rely very much on outside staff. And we also have high staff turnover. In his time my father established a pension fund for the employees staying in the business for their careers; now we celebrate when people have been with us for more than five years.'

I wanted to ask Gerald Voisin about his political career. He entered the States in 1999 as Deputy for St Lawrence. From 2002 he held the important position of President of the Economic Development Committee, an interesting and challenging responsibility as preparations at the time were being made for the change to ministerial government following the recommendation of the Clothier report and the setting up of a Ministry of Economic Development. I asked Gerald about the States and reform. 'I am sure that there does need to be reform in the way that the States are elected, but I did not agree with the Clothier recommendation about removing the Constables from the Assembly. In my view they are some of the wisest people there. And it was a great shame to start paying States Members. What we are seeing now is the emergence of a class of professional politicians and with them have come longer and longer sittings and not a few silly propositions.' And why did he decide to leave the States? 'The business called me: we had made some major investments in it and there were sales targets to hit in order to justify this. I needed to come back and get it right; as well as spending more time with the family since States membership these days is a time-devouring process.'

After having relinquished politics, Gerald Voisin was appointed Chairman of WEB (the Waterfront Enterprise Board) and I wanted to ask him about his controversial removal from that position by the States. This was his reply: 'The States Assembly supported a proposition to remove me on the basis that there was a conflict of interest between my role at WEB and my chairmanship at the time of a local company, Allied Irish Bank (CI) Ltd. It was claimed that there was a conflict because of links between the parent company, Allied Irish Bank Plc based in Ireland, and a preferred developer of WEB called Harcourt Developments Ltd. The local company, Allied Irish Bank (CI) had no dealings or links at all with Harcourt, and even the parent bank in Ireland had no involvement with Harcourt's projects in Jersey. As Chairman of Allied Irish Bank (CI) Ltd, I had nothing to do with Harcourt, and even the States Comptroller and Auditor General reported that I had no conflict of interest and that I had breached no laws or articles of association. Despite this, the States Members lodging the proposition to remove me didn't have the courtesy to contact me and clarify the situation. For the Assembly to remove someone from office for reasons which were clearly not supported by the facts is somewhat worrying. Remember that I had only become Chairman of WEB out of a sense of duty, having been begged to take on the role by the then Chief Minister because the Council of Ministers had fallen out with the previous chairman.'

I ended by asking Gerald, with his business and political antennae, whether he was an optimist about the Island and the future of its finance industry. He replied in this manner: 'Political stability is all-important in a financial jurisdiction, and what worries me is the current vogue by some of being anti-finance. If the finance industry went, then a vital part of our economy would be lost and it would be hard to see that de Gruchy's and ourselves, both trading at the better end of the market, could survive. Yes, I am an optimist, but some of the things that go on in the States Assembly worry me.'

~

Which was established first – de Gruchy's or Voisins? The facts are uncertain: perhaps de Gruchy's first, but then with a possible interruption in its history bestowing the claim on Voisins. As I walked down King Street I had to give more than passing interest to Voisins' rival store where, in its Jersey-owned days, my father-in-law had once been chairman of its board of directors. Architecturally it is the entrance to de Gruchy's arcade that attracts attention, dating from 1883 with its ornate pediment topped by urns and elaborate ironwork. I wandered in and caught up with Cartia, an assistant in the shoe department. She is from Madeira and told me that she had been in Jersey for a year and attracted to the Island, like so many other Portuguese, by having a relative, in her case an uncle, already resident. Was she enjoying her new life here? 'Yes, it's OK, not bad, but housing is so expensive.' With Cartia's confident manner I was not surprised to learn that she had retail experience previously in Portugal. Would she be staying for long in Jersey? 'I don't know,' was her reply. Were her present employers supportive of her and her colleagues? 'Yes, they look after us well.' By now customers were waiting for attention and I took my leave, wandering out into Jersey's main shopping street and towards Charing Cross where I turned up York Street to the Town Hall.

Maurice Boots is more complimentary about this 1872 building than is Brett. Boots describes it in these terms: 'A solidly and carefully detailed ground floor external façade in rusticated local granite supporting a richly detailed French Renaissance first floor above, surmounted by the wholly appropriate mansard roof'. Brett is somewhat more dismissive: 'Not a loveable building, but carries all the bureaucratic gravitas of a French *mairie*'. My mission was not a study of the outside but a chat inside and a few floors up with Peter Noble, the parish of St Helier's Director Technical and Environmental Services.

Peter, born in Carlisle, was brought up in London ('thus the London accent'). He studied civil and structural engineering, ultimately specialising in cold storage and factory building. A job advert for a post in Jersey brought him and his family to the Island in 1977 where he set up a consultancy engineering practice. In 1996 he came to work for the parish of St Helier, taking over from the retiring Town Surveyor. Since then the job and its title have both altered. What then, I asked, were his current responsibilities? 'Basically it is the structural side, the building side, plus the maintenance of the property portfolio. You see, the parish owns buildings worth £55m; it's quite a bit of real estate to look after. And there are responsibilities for the by-roads, the car parks and all the open spaces including the cemeteries and the parks and gardens.'

Simon Crowcroft became Constable in 2001. Had he been a new broom? 'Yes,' replied Peter Noble, 'he has been. He came in and made some drastic cuts as far as management was concerned. Simon can be quite a hard taskmaster, with his philosophy of the money being just enough and no more in order to get the job done. And since he came we now have no chief executive; the Constable is the titular head of a board of directors. There are four of us: municipal services (that's refuse collection, street cleaning, workshops, maintenance of parks and gardens), the HR director, the finance director and myself as director technical and environmental services.'

What were Peter's special headaches? 'The biggest problem is not being responsible for everything that goes on in St Helier. All the parish workforce finds this frustrating. There is this weird and wonderful arrangement where the States are responsible for the administration and therefore the cleansing and maintenance of the main roads and the parishes have responsibility for the by-roads. So we have to liaise with the States and are not free just to go ahead and get on with the job. And the political element comes into it too, with the Council of Ministers getting involved with their Island as opposed to the parish responsibilities. I must say that there's no big duplication problem in all this, and the process of negotiating with the States and the trade union with regard to more rational arrangements does continue.'

Town Hall

~ THE ROYAL SQUARE AND UP ROUGE BOUILLON...

Besides his major St Helier post in the administration of Jersey's largest parish Peter has a number of other interests and activities. He has for some years been a lay reader at St Lawrence parish church and he is involved in the work of the Gideons with their distribution of Bibles to schools and hotels. He is also chairman of the Building Industry Apprenticeship Council which advises Highlands College on relevant matters. He finds time too for an occasional round of golf at Les Mielles. As to his three decades in Jersey, he and his family have no regrets. Indeed his children, now adult, told their parents years ago that they, the parents, were never to move away from the Island.

~

Having left Peter Noble high up in his French Renaissance town hall, I took the few steps back to Charing Cross and climbed the three floors of No.13 to the offices of Meridian Asset Management (C.I.) Ltd to meet and chat with David Mashiter who for many years has had his finger on the pulse of Jersey's finance industry. David, educated at Malvern and then Emmanuel College, Cambridge, where he read Economics, had his first links with the Island when his grandfather moved here in 1951. After university he worked in the research department of London stockbrokers Simon and Coates before coming to Jersey in 1976 to run the investment side of the Royal Trust of Canada's operation here. He left the Royal Trust in 1990 and after a short break set up Meridian Asset Management (C.I.) Ltd which he has headed since its foundation the following year.

I asked David to tell me in simple terms – for my sake in particular – what was the role of his company. This was his reply: 'We provide just one service which is discretionary investment management of a traditional nature. We invest in equities, bonds and cash; we don't invest in hedge funds. It is central to our philosophy that we do not take commission on anything; we get no benefit from dealing or investing in particular securities; everything is completely transparent. We hope that we give our clients a personal service at a rate of charge below the market; we are looking for a long-term relationship with them. You could describe us as a niche business, investing for our clients all over the world: a traditional firm with our income derived from fees and nothing else.'

And the future of the Island's finance industry? 'Jersey faces a very challenging time. We do not have a lot of friends in the world: the EU looks on us with suspicion and the UK tries to exert an indirect influence on us, and Jersey is not big enough to resist some of these pressures. Also there are many challenges from rival financial centres such as the Middle East and Singapore. Take Abu Dhabi, Qatar and Dubai, all with burgeoning finance industries and punching well above their weight because of their immense wealth. We cannot in any way afford to be complacent.' And what of our repute as a finance centre? David's answer was this: 'In my view we are above reproach. The hoops we have to go through are very high indeed, with people sometimes not always wanting to appreciate the considerable level of regulation. Take anti-laundering regulations: strict and sound. Our standards are very, very high.'

In answer to my questions David Mashiter went on to reiterate the point made to me earlier by Gerald Voisin: that the stability of the finance industry depends on the stability of our political system. 'To me this is a huge worry. I look back to the days of Cyril Le Marquand. He was a great and far-sighted statesman and had the finest notion of public service, and there was Colin Powell, a man intellectually in the top class. Those were the glory days. Sadly I consider that we have moved from statesmen to politicians; in the States there is now this confrontational style with the quick sound bite, the instant opinion; it is all far removed from the great stability of former years. Some of today's politicians seem unable to see the bigger picture or appreciate the damage of backbiting and score settling. The fact is that Jersey now needs all the friends it can get, and our current political state damages its image.'

After that bleak appraisal I shifted our conversation onto somewhat less contentious ground – David's involvement in the affairs of the National Trust For Jersey. He has been on its Council for over 20 years and is chairman of its finance committee. 'The work of the National Trust has always held a great appeal for me – the importance of preserving the Island's beautiful scenery and its fine buildings in the face of pressure for development. And the National Trust rightly makes its voice felt as the occasion arises but sensibly resists being against everything, a procedure that would mean no one ever taking any notice of its views. We have a strong chief executive and a clear plan of where we are going. We have resisted becoming too political and we don't pop up with an instant sound bite and an instant opinion. I am very pleased to be involved with the National Trust and glad that I can play this small part in its affairs.'

Finally we came back to finance, and I left David Mashiter with these words of concern ringing in my ears: 'The finance industry is so important for Jersey. If it upped and went, then we would be in a terrible state; there is nothing else substantial to support us. Finance is vital, and our politicians should be doing everything to ensure that it flourishes and the industry stays here. If finance goes, then there is nothing to replace it.'

~

Sand Street and Seaton Place are hardly St Helier's most charming thoroughfares, but at the end of the latter as one reaches Gloucester Street is Jersey's Opera House. The present building is actually a 1922 reconstruction of the earlier theatre, opened by Lillie Langtry in 1900 but burnt down in 1921. Thus it dates from the best period of late Victorian and early Edwardian theatre and opera design, and both its exterior and interior, following a further major restoration in the years 1997 to 2000, reflect this fact. Some have questioned this fairly recent £5m investment, wondering whether a new multi-purpose auditorium might have been a better solution, but local sentiment is strong for this much-loved building. I went inside to meet up with its Theatre Director, Jasmine Hendry.

Jasmine told me that after school her ambition was to go into social work but she went off the idea when the contract was discussed and it was stated that the cost of private treatment would be covered not if but when she had a breakdown. 'Maybe social work was not for me. Instead I increasingly became involved in arts administration.' After various other appointments she was principal arts officer in Oldham, in charge of five venues there before becoming chief executive of Chester's Gateway Theatre. She came to her present position in Jersey in January 2007.

What, I asked her, were her feelings about the Opera House? 'It's a beautiful building and I welcomed the challenge of being its custodian and ensuring its survival. I am passionate about my spaces and if I had not liked the auditorium, then this would not have been the job for me. Instead I fell in love with it; it is relatively intimate, seating 625, and wherever you sit you can see and hear reasonably well. Yes, it is true that you can't change the structure for different performances; it is what it is. And ideally there should be more space for in-house workshops and classes. Perhaps one day the funding will allow this.'

How did Jasmine view her mission at the Opera House? 'We are here to provide a variety of entertainment for the people of the Island and we actually run the operation with only 13 full-time members of staff. And the perennial question is this: what do people in any venue want to come and see? We produce three brochures of programmes a year; if you pick up each of those three brochures and in each there is one thing you would like to see at the Opera House, then we are hitting the target. It's quite a challenge in an island of only 90,000, requiring a balanced programme with around 250 performances a year to keep us financially viable.'

I then referred to controversies, partly financial, before Jasmine Hendry took up her post. What was the degree of States funding? 'We get around £442,000 per annum in subsidy and the box office take is around £200,000. The subsidy, by the way, is not huge compared with other places in the UK. Yes, the funding could be more generous, allowing us properly to maintain the fabric of the theatre, but the subsidy and the box office receipts just about cover our current outgoings. We like bringing over West End shows: *Hello, Dolly* was a very slick production with fantastic sets and costumes. We break even by balancing our programmes and come out all right at the end of the financial year. True, it is tough: the Siberian opera company was a very successful engagement, but remember it had 45 in the cast, an orchestra of 45 and the cost of bringing over their three 40-foot trucks was £10,000. And don't forget the accommodation and travel cost of 90 people.'

Jasmine had not known Jersey before her arrival in early 2007. She and her partner are discovering the delights of Jersey's beaches and coastal walks. The *Jersey Evening Post* is, she tells me, essential reading. And the Island's system of government? 'I would like, separate from Education and Sports, for us to have a Minister of Culture.'

~

Across the road from the Opera House is Jersey's General Hospital. Architecturally it is surely something of a mess, with the decision made decades ago for it to be redeveloped on its current site rather than replaced by a completely new complex constructed somewhere in the Island's precious countryside. It was originally completed as a hospital in 1768 and then used as a barracks. A plaque on its outer wall indicates this:

> **Battle of Jersey**
> **January 6th 1781**
> The five companies of the 78th Regiment (Highlanders)
> which distinguished themselves in the market place
> were billeted in this hospital

It was then reopened as a hospital in 1793 and burned down in 1859. The austere and dignified principal front to Gloucester Street is thus Victorian, with its somewhat lonely and formidable gatehouse adjacent to the street, built, says Brett, 'in Victorian neo-Norman style'. Around this core there is a variety of modern additions, in Brett's words 'none offensive but none better than mediocre'. Part of the trouble must surely be the variety of facing materials used: the original building is of natural granite; the post-war nurses' home has locally made pink facing blocks; the Gwyneth Huelin wing has locally made smooth white blocks; and the exterior of the nine-story building built in the early 1960s and overlooking The Parade has imported facing bricks. I put aside these aesthetic considerations and went up in the smart lift of the Peter Crill Building to meet Mike Pollard, Chief Executive of the States' Health and Social Services Department.

Mike grew up in the slums of Yorkshire's West Riding – in Wakefield - and speaks graphically about the opportunities that came his way. 'I was the first person on our street to get O-levels and the first person to go to university. The careers advice given me at my secondary modern school was information about a vacancy for a coffin liner at the local co-op undertakers. Instead I went on to Stirling University, gained a degree in sociology and industrial relations and then did post-graduate research in Edinburgh.' Various posts in health administration followed including that of chief officer since 1991. He was appointed to his present position in January 2004 and took up his post in the following May.

General Hospital

Aware of the complex nature of the General Hospital's buildings, I asked Mike Pollard if the plant worked? 'Yes, it is true that there are eyesore areas to be resolved, but there are some nice architectural features as well, with the Jersey fondness for granite. But modern hospitals require massive flexibility and their walls are all stud partitions. Here instead we have walls that are two foot thick; every time we put in computers, vital for modern clinical work, we have to drill through the stone and the reinforced concrete floors. So there is to some extent a lack of flexibility. Medicine these days moves fast. One day in the future patients will be in en-suite, individual rooms; so we are spending millions of pounds redesigning wards, and this will bring about a big increase in the number of single rooms, with consequent benefits concerning hospital-acquired infections.'

What, I asked, were the particular problems in running a general hospital in Jersey? This was Mike Pollard's response: 'A hospital requires an infrastructure, however big or small it is – x-ray, medical records, an ICT department, diagnostic pathology services and so on. Such services can serve a population of 80,000 or 300,000. Whatever your size, you have got to have them. Thus the infrastructure costs in Jersey are necessarily much higher than for a hospital serving a bigger catchment area in the UK. And another of our problems concerns medical specialisation: here in Jersey there is not enough morbidity, illness or injury to keep specialists upskilled. In modern medicine there is an equation around successful outcome and numbers of operations performed. So we do have to send a lot of work off-Island with all the anxieties and problems for our patients, away from family and having to go elsewhere for life-saving treatment.'

I also wanted to know how in the absence of UK league tables, Jersey's hospital was kept up to scratch. 'It is true,' Mike replied, 'that we lack predators; if this were King's College Hospital in south London, then down the road there is the competition of Guy's and St Thomas's. But here we avoid becoming insidiously comfortable by various procedures such as peer review – by distinguished independent people from outside; and each doctor receives continuous professional development, with all our consultants having to be members of their relevant clinical network elsewhere.'

Mike made a further observation that I, with my past headmastering experience, could appreciate. 'As with schools you can tell within minutes walking round a hospital what is the true spirit and feel of the place. The General Hospital is the biggest institution in Jersey, and those who work here are held high in the affections of the community. Yes, all human life is here and there are the occasional tragedies. The public sometimes think that doctors and nurses get used to dealing with death. That's not so. We've had a number of difficult deaths this year and for the staff dealing with them it is very tough. I am reassured by that; there is no sense of being blasé.'

We finished our chat with my asking Mike Pollard, newcomer to Jersey just a few years ago, about his new environment. His answer was reassuring: 'I love the place. Whereas UK society can be anonymous, here it is wonderfully benign and inclusive while not being claustrophobic. As a family, with my wife HR director for the States of Jersey and a daughter at JCG and son at Victoria College, we have quickly come to love the Island. I put out the flags on Liberation Day. We try to demonstrate an affinity with those who are indigenous, taking nothing for granted and feeling privileged to live here and be part of Jersey's community.'

~

After I left Mike Pollard I wandered through the hospital and, feeling something of an intruder, made my way up in the lift to Plémont ward. A young doctor there, with stethoscope at the ready round his neck, claimed to be too busy for a word with me. I was more fortunate with staff nurse Pamela Eugenio who took me into a day room, sat me down and told me something of her career and what brought her to Jersey. From the Philippines she came here in June 2007, having done her initial nursing training at home and then completing an additional course in Guernsey, having been there for three and a half years. With the RAF Red Arrows rehearsing for the annual air show and 'buzzing' us overhead with shattering noise (hard luck for the sick patients!) I asked Pamela why she had chosen the Channel Islands? 'This has been an opportunity for me to expand my experience and my knowledge and has allowed me to see something of Europe as well. I had never heard of Jersey and Guernsey before I came. I'm glad to be here rather than, say, in London. I grew up in a city and the islands are nice and quiet.' (At this point in our conversation the RAF did another ear-splitting run over our heads.). Had Patricia, I asked, visited much of the Island since coming? Her answer indicated that there was still much to see: 'No, not yet, but I have stayed in Grouville and been to Gorey.'

~

It was time for me to explore The Parade, that pleasant and spacious triangular open space with its lawns and garden, its Don Memorial and its seemingly well-patronised open-air café, a recent reincarnation of the area's public lavatories. The statue to Lieutenant-Governor General Don is impressive and flanked by two breech-loading 32-pounder cannons of 1862. An inscription tells us more:

> General Sir George Don (1756-1832) served in Jersey 1792-1793, 1806-1809 and 1810-1814. On 21st May 1810 presented by the militia with gold-hilted sword now in Edinburgh War Museum. Left Jersey in 1814 to become Governor of Gibraltar. Died 1st January 1832 and buried on site of Gibraltar Cathedral. Monument unveiled 29th October 1885.

Here he is life-size in a dashing and very long cloak and flanked not only by the cannons but also by rather larger-than-life-size statues of Ceres and Mercury, the former puzzlingly scratching her head. And why did the Island wait more than fifty years in order to commemorate him in such a grand manner?

The Parade also has more: a head and shoulders bust commemorating Philippe Baudains, Connétable of St Helier in the late 19th and early 20th centuries, and benches for office workers and visitors enjoying their cigarettes, reading their papers and eating their sandwiches. The benches are also the haunt of some of the less fortunate members of Jersey's society, and I plucked up courage at this hour of 10 a.m. and approached three men, with tins of lager in their hands and sufficient

further supplies to last them for some time ahead in plastic bags at their feet. I told them that I was writing a book about St Helier and asked whether I could chat with them and record our conversation. In a friendly and ironic manner, one of them asked me for identification: 'Are you the police?' 'No,' I replied, 'As you can see I'm far too old for that.' Martin told me that he was a Glaswegian and had been twenty years in Jersey. He stayed overnights at the Shelter in Kensington Place and that had been his place to sleep for a year and a half. Why, I asked, did he not have a job? His response was this: 'I was a roofer, but I'm not working now. I got knocked down a year ago.' I turned to Robert, also from Glasgow. He told me that he was a carpenter by trade and did not work because the taxman took away one's wages. When I asked him whether Jersey treated him fairly, he answered strangely: 'Here's the total truth. Young boys and young ladies walk the streets. The bottom line is this: society is terrible with Jersey children on the streets with nowhere to go. Why are they treated like this?' I asked Robert and Martin whether they were in touch with their families. Martin told me that he had a daughter and two sons; he was not in contact with them and his daughter would not speak to him. Robert replied: 'My mother always told me that no news is good news; I say that if they hear nothing, then everything is fine.'

Robert now returned to his previous theme, introducing me to Paul who was sitting nearby. Robert continued: 'Look at Paul, aged twenty-seven and fallen into the trap that society has set for him. He's a young Jerseyman. As for me I walked out of my beautiful home, packed my bags and just went. Within two weeks Scottish society provided a home to accommodate me and two of my children. However, in Jersey these kids don't get accommodation. And I don't give a f*** if they're Portuguese, Spanish, pink, yellow, green. Jersey doesn't look after them. It's wrong.' I then turned to Paul who had been listening to this and he confirmed that he was Jersey born and bred. He continued: 'I was a plumber, a bricklayer and a ganger. I moved back from a time in London and couldn't get a job. My biggest disadvantage is that I haven't got a driving licence. Before I went to London I was earning £14 an hour. Now I would be lucky to be earning £12 an hour because of all the foreign workers here.' In fact his appearance suggested to me that he was probably quite unfit for work.

Not unexpectedly Robert's, Martin's and Paul's answers to my questions had hardly been coherent, and I had my own instincts as to why these men, two in their forties and one in his twenties, were out of work and out of society. It was a reminder to me that Jersey, with one of the highest standards of living in the world, has its share of misfits and dropouts, dependent on alcohol as they pass their days drinking and smoking on the Parade benches before the Shelter opens to receive them for the night.

~

After my heightened chats with Robert, Martin and Paul, it was time for a little solace, on offer at All Saints, the church overlooking The Parade and well known to me since I am its organist. Brett has some architectural observations concerning it: 'A small chapel of ease, of modestly correct classical design inside and out, spoiled outside by the ubiquitous rendering and inside by the excess of pale oak... not at all in keeping with the period or the style of the building'. It was constructed in 1835 to take the overflow from St Helier's parish church (those happier days for the Church of England when its pews were full) and built on the site of a cholera graveyard. Indeed in recent years when a car park was created at the front, Andy Errington-Rennell of undertakers Pitcher and Le Quesne was called in to supervise necessary exhumations and reburials.

All Saints, The Parade

Waiting to talk to me on a weekday morning was the All Saints administrator, Jackie Edwards. Jackie, a private secretary by qualification and profession, was christened at All Saints in 1956 and married here in 1980. She filled me in: 'You see, my parents ran a guest house in Patriotic Street, where the prison once was and where the car park now is, and from an early age I attended the Sunday School here. After marriage our children also came along to the Sunday School. It was perhaps eighteen years ago that I offered to help out and started co-ordinating what we now call the junior church.' And how did she become administrator? 'When Geoff Houghton became vicar he was looking for someone to manage the paperwork. I was on the church committee and my boys were now at school; I had the time and offered to help. The job has grown over the years and I am now the administrator not only of All Saints but also of St Simon's and, when Geoff became Rector of Trinity as well, I started to do the administrative work there also.'

Jackie is a committed person and she went on to tell me about Open The Book of which she is the co-ordinator. 'We take the Bible into the Island's primary schools. It's for the key stage 1 pupils. We keep it simple, going in and doing a simple ten-minute assembly presentation, sharing a story, having a short prayer and finishing with an action song. We are ecumenical – Anglicans, Methodists, Salvation Army, Roman Catholics – which is great.' Jackie is also involved with Jersey's ecumenical Christian Unity Group which recently sent a team to Kenya to help build a clinic. In October 2007 she went out to check on the project. 'The primary school children in this village on the eastern shores of Lake Victoria seemed to go all day without a meal. So we bought some fields and started a feeding programme for the provision of a simple school lunch. I found the Kenyans' faith extraordinary, a faith that God will guide them through each day. It was amazing and humbling to meet with them. They seem to have it so right faith-wise.'

Jackie and I then chatted about the Church of England's current state and how it seems to be its evangelical wing that flourishes. She made the observation that at All Saints 'we have had people who have settled in this church because they have been elsewhere and found them too happy-clappy. It is surely good that in Jersey we have this diversity of different church practices. The evangelical forms of service don't work for me; I find the experience uncomfortable. I suppose it's down to my traditional church upbringing. I love what we do at All Saints with my family's long association with it. I think there's something for everybody here.'

~

It was time to resume my journey and, before heading up Rouge Bouillon, I strolled along Cheapside which is a part of Town with its cafés and shops closely associated with St Helier's significant Portuguese community. Numbers one to seven are occupied by Alfonso Superstore and Newsagents and I made my way through the shop's packed aisles, past its butchery department and up the stairs to an office where I was welcomed by owner Manuel Alfonso and manager Isabel Cerca. Manuel's story is an enterprising one; he came to Jersey in 1989 at the age of twenty-three, having opened his first business in Venezuela at the age of seventeen. He continued: 'My profession is that of a butcher; I am Jersey's first Portuguese businessman. When I first came here I worked on a farm and did part-time work in a Market butcher's on Saturdays. Then they wanted me fulltime. I then became a wholesale butcher with my own van and I bought the butcher's shop in Cheapside in 1994. The police got worried since the customers had to queue thirty-deep in the street because the shop was both small and popular. Now it is big; I bought the whole property and expanded it. In 1994 I also opened the minimarket and butcher's shop in Minden Street. There was no Portuguese bakery and no Portuguese bread, so I acquired a bakery; it's a wholesale bakery business as well now. Later I bought the freehold of Minden Street and opened a first-floor restaurant. In 2007 I sold that property and I now concentrate on my Cheapside business.' I remarked on Manuel's butchery counter below where we were chatting, and he gave me a surprising reply: 'I have my own pork. I own a farm in St Peter's Valley. I have 300 pigs there. You see, I am from the countryside in Madeira; at home we had pigs, cows, goats lambs.'

I now turned to Isabel who first came to Jersey in 1993. I wanted to know more about the Island's Portuguese community. I mentioned her perfect English and she told me how she had learned English at school in Madeira but her grasp of the language was not good enough. 'When I first came to Jersey I worked on a farm. I remember getting on a bus and telling the driver that I wanted to go into the city. I improved my English by doing a course at Highlands College. It was my means of competing for jobs along with local people.'

I also wondered whether Jersey was sufficiently welcoming to the Portuguese community and about the problems of integration. Isabel chose to answer my question in this way: 'I was talking to a lady who teaches English to Portuguese people. She had written in the *JEP* with her e-mail address, proposing socialising activities, children getting together and so on. I took this up and e-mailed her. Now a lot of Portuguese people read the paper and, when I met her later, she told me that she had only received two e-mail responses, one from me and the other from Radio Jersey. The thing is this: so many Portuguese people come to Jersey to work hard and do not have much time for socialising. Perhaps a Sunday morning if not working or before going off to work. And the place they go to is the coffee shop. That's why Portuguese come here to Cheapside, perhaps between 6 and 8 in the morning. They come to meet friends, have their coffee, and the builders pick up some of their staff from here. It's a Portuguese custom to meet others for coffee and to have a chat.'

I wondered whether Manuel and Isabel would spend the rest of their busy lives in Jersey, or would they perhaps go home one day. Manuel replied in this way: 'Jersey is good and safe. I also like the weather. This is the weather for me.' And my last question to my enterprising hosts was this: might it be good if there were a Portuguese deputy in the States Assembly. Manuel gave a laugh: 'In a couple of years' time, I'll be there.'

~

~ THE ROYAL SQUARE AND UP ROUGE BOUILLON...

Rouge Bouillon, a busy section of the St Helier ring road, is essentially a Victorian/Regency thoroughfare. But one has to look carefully to see what remains in this street of once-grand villas. Brett is particularly rude about the Savoy Hotel, opposite the police headquarters. He writes this: 'Observe how merrily the hotel keeper, having ruined everything else, has retained the stonework at the corner pilasters and the entablature with the nicely carved date 1840. This was once a very handsome large stone house – Beau Sejour, the Governor's office. It is kind of the owners to allow one to guess its past'. Ouch!

Before venturing along the road I had business to conduct fifty yards into Parade Road at BBC Radio Jersey. I was on my way to meet and chat with Roger Bara, well-known and popular local broadcaster. As I approached, a group of people emerged from a posh limousine, making, as I was, for the BBC's front door and reception area. Who among them, I puzzled, was the lady whose face I immediately recognised? And then the penny dropped: I was in the presence of that great opera diva, Dame Kiri Te Kanawa, here to answer questions on the radio preceding her concert at Fort Regent the following evening. So for a few minutes in reception Dame Kiri and I rubbed shoulders while she waited for her interviewer to collect her and I waited for Roger Bara. Roger arrived and, as he and I climbed the stairs to a quiet room at the top of the building, I remarked that it was not often that I met two such popular public figures and at the same time. Roger gave a modest chuckle.

My first question to Roger Bara was about his surname. He had a fascinating story to tell: 'My father was Polish and Mum came from Silesia, that part of Poland which became Germany. During the last war Dad escaped from a POW camp in Romania, ended up in Alexandria, got on a boat, landed in Marseilles and got out the day that Hitler invaded France and arrived in England. He was then stationed in various places – a horrendous time for him in what was in effect a foreign country. Eventually he gained British naturalization and went back to get Mum – which is another amazing story. They set up home in Hertfordshire. I am a boy from Royston and lived there until I left school.'

Roger went on to tell me about his post-school career: 'Music was my main love. I could read music before I could properly read. My music teacher wanted me to become a classical pianist, but then the Beatles arrived on the scene and I moved to a more modern style and improvisation. Eventually I went pro as a musician. In 1981 I was directing a show in Guernsey, and impresario Dick Ray brought it over to Caesar's Palace at Grève de Lecq. So I ended up in the Island, intending to be here for a couple of years or so. With two young children we then decided to stay. Shows at Caesar's Palace and the Opera House and running my own recording studio became my life and then I started working on radio, doing bits and pieces for BBC Radio Jersey. In the early '90s I did a swap: music became my hobby and radio my career.'

I wanted Roger to tell me about the 12 noon Radio Jersey phone-in (which I compulsively turn on if I am in the car at that time), known by at least some as the moan-in, with its regular ringers-up including Bridget, Emile, Tony and others. I asked whether it was Roger's favourite programme and received a surprising reply: 'No, it's not. There are no sound delays and I have constantly to be listening for slander and unproven accusations. I actually get a fair amount of hate mail because most people that call up are anti-establishment and against what is happening in the Island. To balance things up I have necessarily got to air the pro-establishment point of view, and this gets translated as my own opinion. So I can't find it a relaxing hour, and it comes at the end of a long shift that sometimes starts with me clocking in at 4 a.m.'

And local radio? What was the BBC's mission here? Roger's answer was forthright: 'It is no different from John Reith's philosophy – information, education, entertainment. Our problem at Radio Jersey is this: we are funded as a very small local station, but the job we do is the same as national radio. It's a very tight budget and with no resources to spare for investigative journalism. You ask whether the BBC should be in local radio at all, and my answer to that is this: BBC Radio Jersey gets the best percentage listening figures in the British Isles. If there were no call for what we broadcast, then people would not listen to us. And we are impartial: our manual of guidance is that thick; the rules are very thorough; we can't accept a dinner invitation anywhere in the Island unless we pay for it ourselves. People bring goodies for us here and we are not allowed to accept them.' Was that a little conspiratorial wink that Roger gave me as he stated this? I did not wish to enquire further.

Roger keeps up his other interests too: he is patron of Jersey Sports Association for the Disabled and he is still a professional musician directing the music for the Green Room pantomimes. And his thoughts about Jersey and his nearly three decades in the Island? He still resents the housing qualifications and the many years of his professional and charitable activities before he and his family were able to acquire decent housing at a decent price. And how might Jersey change? 'I resent the fact that we lack a decent mass transit system. I would love to see trams and I would love the Island to become fully organic. Why not electric cars? We could blaze a trail here.'

And our Island way of life? 'It is both unique and endearing and at the same time quaint and troubling. Yes, things are sometimes swept under the carpet, and it can take ten years longer than elsewhere for change to be effected. We could be radical and get away with it, but I sense that there is no stomach for it, and even after nearly three decades here I still don't feel I have the right to be too forward. Yes, I would like to see trams, an infrastructure for future generations. And what about a bridge to France? I'm all for it: catching a TGV train from Gorey Pier Station and getting easily to the rest of Europe. That's incidentally one of the great things about Jersey: I adore living close to France.'

~

I returned to Rouge Bouillon, noticing a fairly modern tower block across the road and conscious as I had been elsewhere in Town that large areas of St Helier were redeveloped in the 1960s, with the then fashionable high-rise flats taking the place of too many demolished 18th and 19th century buildings. The Ambulance Station further along the road was built in 1981 and is in no way architecturally related to the original Regency/Victorian domestic character of the area. It is a steel-framed structure and, in Boots's words, 'a low-key fairly anonymous treatment'. I dropped in for a chat with the about-to-retire Chief Ambulance Officer, John Moulin.

John is Jersey-born. He left school at fifteen and went into the motor trade, doing a full five-year apprenticeship. During this time he became involved in the St John Ambulance and this led to a career change in 1980 when, in his words, he 'replaced the motor car for people'. In fact the States ambulance service grew out of the St John Ambulance, with a final break coming in 1976 followed by the move to this Rouge Bouillon site in 1981. Having joined the service, John progressed to station officer in 1985, assistant chief officer in 1987 and into his current position in 1993.

I asked about the scope of the Ambulance Service's work. John replied: 'We have four distinct elements – the front-line ambulance service (with the sirens, stripes and lights), the patient transport services, the control centre (for both the fire and ambulance services) and we maintain the full vehicle fleet for the States Health department.' And training for the ambulance crews? 'All this is done predominantly in the UK. The frontline staff first become ambulance technicians with a ten-week training course in the UK which includes emergency driver training. Then they have to complete a minimum of eighteen months on the road to gain experience before they are considered ready for paramedic training, having to pass an assessment before going forward. They then attend a seven-week course in the UK followed by a further four-week hospital phase back in Jersey; and after that they go through various updates to comply with local protocols. There are also many weeks of private study to complete during this period. We're also extremely lucky to have fantastic support here in Jersey from the General Hospital and the consultant staff.'

I wondered whether the ambulance service in an island such as Jersey made special demands. 'All our training,' said John Moulin, 'mirrors that of the UK. Isolation, it is true, does make a difference. There could be skills erosion and this is countered with constant retraining. Also, unlike the UK, we are obviously unable to call on services from elsewhere such as a neighbouring county if there were an incident in which we might be overwhelmed. We meet this with our ambulance support unit and its thirty volunteers, well trained and highly enthusiastic. And of course we also work closely with St John Ambulance; they're on our radio system and form an integral part of our major incident plan.'

John reminded me how front-line ambulance work had changed since he joined the service nearly three decades ago. 'Since around 1990 paramedic training has become the norm, and around 75% of our staff are paramedic-trained. The techniques used and the level of service provided for the public are far, far greater now.' And John added that he had introduced female staff into the service in 1987/8 ('a fine development' was his description) and now constituting 45% of his personnel.

I wanted to know how his emergency staff reacted to the stress of their job. 'Yes, people die, lose limbs, suffer terrible injuries, commit suicide. And there are cot deaths, other unexplained deaths and assaults. We have a counselling service in place. There's no gender issue here: the men can take all this to heart as much as women; they all can suffer equally. Support in these circumstances comes very much from informal debriefing: going into the duty room; everybody knowing what has happened; offloading some of it onto one's colleagues. And, yes, there's quite a bit of black humour as well, and that undoubtedly relieves pressure. In addition there can be off-the-record discussions with staff and, if we detect special issues, then we can go to the professional counselling stage. Staff are not blasé, not hardened to incidents, but there is this inbuilt ability to support one another.'

John Moulin concluded by telling me that he did not have a queue of troubled people at his door. 'We have a very low turnover and that is surely a good indicator. The ambulance service is dealing with human beings, and there is much reward and job satisfaction in that. You can walk away at the end of a shift and say, yes, I had a good day. And if the day has been trying and tough, then there is also a sense of achievement in a job well done.'

~

Across the road from the Ambulance Station are the States of Jersey Police. The headquarters complex consists of a 1967 block faced with pink artificial granite and black granite slabs, described by Brett as 'a reasonably discreet exercise', and a converted grammar school dating from earlier times. Relocation to a new building across the road is a possibility. I turned to someone I know well socially to fill me in as to whether a Jersey policeman's lot is or is not a happy one. Police Sergeant Colin Belsey and I are both change ringers at St John's, one of the only two churches in the Island (the other is St Mark's in David Place) that have peals of bells able to be rung in the traditional English campanological manner. We do not normally talk about police matters over our post-practice pints; now was my chance to find out more.

~ THE ROYAL SQUARE AND UP ROUGE BOUILLON...

Colin came to Jersey from Sussex in 1981 as a trainee manager for Woolworth's. He married, decided to stay in the Island and joined the States police in late 1982, doing his ten-week training at Ashford in Kent (in these days it is now completed in Jersey). He sketched out his career to me: 'I started as a constable walking the beat. I then had six months out at St Brelade's before doing four years in the traffic department, an excellent grounding being called out to all sorts of incidents. There then followed a spell at the airport and harbour with the Special Branch and a long period of nine years with the Fraud Squad when our investigations took me to New York, the British Virgin Islands and Brittany. In 2002 I was promoted to sergeant and my current duties are those of custody: being responsible for the detention and treatment of prisoners. I have to make the decision about the need for detention; their human rights must be considered and each prisoner has to be risk-assessed, with possible self-harming in mind. Some prisoners have to be cell-guarded; nobody wants the tragedy of a death in custody.' I asked Colin about numbers. 'We have twelve police cells, and these may be filled on a Friday or a Saturday night. On average we have in excess of 3000 prisoners a year. Yes, it's a high-pressure job and a challenge. I get to meet a lot of not always the nicest people, but some do say when they leave, "Thanks for the way you have dealt with this" and I appreciate that.'

What, I wondered had been the most alarming incident in Colin's full police career? 'It was a domestic incident at First Tower and the inspector and I thought that the guy, as he came out of the door towards us, had a gun. We jumped back over a wall in what seemed a stand-off siege situation. It was frightening at the time, but the gun turned out to be a baseball bat.'

Sergeant Belsey went on to tell me something of Jersey's special police problems. 'We have 247 officers; that's our established strength. And perhaps people don't realise that we have national responsibilities here: we have to provide our own firearms unit, our own drugs unit, our own commercial/financial crimes unit, our professional standards unit and so on. Unlike the UK we cannot call on neighbouring forces to help out; we've got to be self-sufficient and possibly more multi-skilled than police elsewhere.'

And Jersey's honorary police system? 'It has far more advantages than disadvantages, and the parish hall enquiry is an efficient way of dealing with minor offences – the modern and more acceptable equivalent to the old police clip on the ear. At times the honoraries are invaluable. If the States police are extended, say, on a Friday night, can we afford to go and deal with cows loose on a lane in St Mary? Instead we phone the centenier and the constable's officers will be called out to deal with the incident. With my custody job I am dealing with the honoraries all the time, and most of the centeniers are absolutely excellent. Long may the system flourish!'

Colin's career in the police is shortly coming to an end and he fancies a complete change with a move to the UK and the possibility of becoming a funeral director. Would he have regrets about leaving the Island? 'Jersey has given me a great living, but I do like wide-open spaces and as an English chap I do find it claustrophobic. It's a lovely island and it does have some problems such as a bit of racial tension, with Portuguese and Poles, for example, paying out for small bed-sits, a lot of money for some fairly squalid accommodation. Are there too many coming into Jersey? Is the Island becoming over-developed? Will it be another Hong Kong in fifty years' time? And youth problems are also worrying with a potential increase in the misuse of drugs and alcohol.'

We had come to the end of our conversation and I asked Colin whether he wanted to get anything else onto the tape. This was his response: 'Don't you want to know about *Bergerac*?' Yes, I did, and Colin continued: 'When the programme was being filmed over here, the States police were used as extras. On our days off we would turn up, lie in the sunshine, be called to do a scene and then go back to lie in the sunshine again. We were able to make use of the TV canteen (no expense spared with its lobster, crab and prawns), and we'd collect £100 for the day's work, and this was a lot of money in 1984. In due course we would be able to see ourselves when the programmes were screened. On my police training course, because of the Jersey *Bergerac* connection, I was known as Berg Belsey. Happy days!'

~

Behind Jersey's police headquarters lies its fire station. Its main building was built in 1912-13 as the Town Arsenal and reopened for the Fire and Rescue Service in 1955. The four large openings on the ground floor with their enormous granite lintels once housed four howitzers and four Maxim guns, with 270 men and supporting equipment also accommodated. And now in these bays? Four fire engines, not quite as big as some UK models, chosen so that they fit these lofty portals. It was just after 6 p.m. and I was on my way to meet Andrew Moisan, Crew Manager (the old nomenclature was Leading Fireman), who with his watch of ten personnel was coming on to start a long night shift until 9 a.m. in the morning. There was a busy hum about the place with equipment being checked in readiness for the three or four calls that might on average be expected in the following fifteen-hour shift. Andrew took me upstairs to a big boardroom-cum-museum, throwing open as we passed it a door bearing red-painted warnings concerning what was on the other side – the pole and the drop down to the ground floor, the firemen's traditional means of descent to the tenders below.

Andrew Moisan has done thirty years in the service, but this Jersey-born firefighter was before that a soldier, a euphonium player in the band of the Royal Ordnance Corps. He told me about his job interview with the then chief fire

~ THE ROYAL SQUARE AND UP ROUGE BOUILLON...

officer: 'I was asked what qualifications I had and I told him that I had an A-level in music which I had done at the Army's music school, Kneller Hall. Fortunately he still took me on and I have found it over all these years such a rewarding job. It has always been a pleasure for me to come to work.'

This is officially the States of Jersey Fire and Rescue Service, with inshore boats for operations involving those trapped on rocks and similar incidents. 'Actually,' Andrew added, 'we save more lives from the sea than from fires.' And besides it is not only cliff rescues but also traffic accidents with the firefighters having the necessary cutting equipment. 'It's all to do with our main mission – saving life.'

Tonight's Crew Manager then told me something of the set-up: 'There are four watches – red, white, blue and green – and people generally stay in those watches. A camaraderie builds up; we're each a little family really; in dicey situations your life can be in the hands of your mates; you depend on each other; and we become fairly close muckers.' I wanted to know whether there was any element of boredom in the job, waiting for the calls to come in. Andrew replied: 'We don't get a chance to be bored. There are all the checks to be done, with the breathing apparatus and so on. On the night shift we do have a stand-down period but if a call comes in we are out in two minutes. If there's a major fire and the whole watch goes to it, then in come the part-time retained firefighters to stand by in the station if there were another call elsewhere in the Island. They I don't envy: they may be called in by their pagers, getting as tired and dirty at four in the morning as us. But we go home at nine o'clock and they go off to work.'

Jersey's fire service faces the same problem as the police and ambulance organisations: there is no neighbouring town or county to be called on for help in a big emergency. 'We're on our own; our coverage has to be complete and totally professional. When there's a major fire such as the ones in the past at the Hotel de France and more recently at Broadlands in St Peter, with its complications of cyclinders exploding, then for something that size and for an incident such as a plane crash we have what's called a Code Amber, when every firefighter in the Island would be involved.'

As with the ambulance staff I wondered how firefighters coped with traumatic and stressful situations – perhaps a terrible road accident. Andrew's answer was similar to that of the Chief Ambulance Officer: 'There's an element of black humour which gets us through, and that is often the way of dealing with it, especially for the more junior chaps seeing horrendous things. Anything involving children can be very harrowing. One is upset; we all have children; but we have a way of getting over it, not dwelling on it too much. It's part of the job.'

Andrew Moisan's retirement (it has to happen at fifty-five years of age) is not too far off. What, I asked, was he going to do then; perhaps take up the euphonium once more? 'Possibly; I still get that surge of excitement and nostalgia when I see and hear the Island of Jersey band. But I am also a great collector of Jersey books and I'm going to open a little antique shop in Colomberie.'

I had found our chat fascinating with such an enthusiast for his profession, and my fascination was not over as I was then shown the museum with its medals, memorabilia, old equipment and photographs of firemen of a previous era. We then went down to the ground floor and Andrew gave me a tour: the gleaming vehicles, engines warmed and ready for immediate action, the inshore dinghies also prepared for an instant summons, the equipment of the various watches systematically and neatly hanging on the walls. My final impressions as I said my thanks and farewell were these: surely this was a life-saving contribution to the community of the greatest discipline, dedication and efficiency. As with the ambulance staff across the road, I sensed that the Island is fortunate indeed to have such streamlined and utterly modern emergency services.

~

I had one final call to make at the end of this my second 'journey' round St Helier. Leaving the police station I turned right and reached the roundabout where Queen's Road meets Rouge Bouillon. Here stands the architecturally somewhat unpretentious Norfolk Lodge Hotel. I had made an arrangement to talk with Paul Okumu whose acquaintance I had made the previous Sunday as I stood at the back of All Saints church having a restorative cup of tea following my stint at the organ console. Norfolk Lodge is one of the Morvan hotels and Paul works in its office there in charge of the reservations for the group. And I had already met his wife Beatrice, assistant manager at Norfolk Lodge and, as I arrived, dispensing advice and assistance to guests from behind the reception desk. Paul was born in a remote village in western Kenya, went to Nairobi for his secondary education and then on to college where he studied and qualified in tourism. After that he spent several years working for Kenya Airways.

How had Paul and his wife arrived in Jersey? He told me: 'The Jersey hospitality representatives came out to Nairobi to recruit graduates from my particular college. That is how we heard of the opportunities here and I came over in March 2003. No, I had never left Africa before. This is my fifth season working for Morvan Hotels. We are here on work permits and the regulation is that we stay for a maximum of nine months and then go home for a minimum of three.'

What, I asked, did Paul and Beatrice know of Jersey before they arrived? 'It was rather exciting. Groups of fellow graduates would go and work in the US at Disneyworld and send back photos. Jersey turned out to be somewhat different – to our pleasant surprise. Indeed it has been more than we expected and we have found lovely people here.'

One of the strengths for Paul has been his involvement with churches in St Helier. 'I found the Church of Scotland close to our place of work and also got to know Geoff Houghton, the vicar of All Saints. But here's the difference: back home you walk into a church and the young ones are in the majority; over here it is the old ones that are in the majority. Yes, the churches in Kenya are more lively and active.' Paul keeps in touch with other Kenyans in Jersey and has contributed to the work of some of our church charities. 'The Jersey community have been very kind to us, very welcoming. That for us has been a bonus and certainly more than we expected.'

I asked Paul a rather difficult question: had he and his wife experienced any racial prejudice in Jersey? His firm answer was in the negative. And Beatrice, first a member of the waiting staff, then receptionist and now assistant manager, has been very much in the front line and experienced no problems of that sort. Paul added: 'Morvan Hotels have been very, very good to us. We feel as though we are part of the family. In the office there is no consciousness that I am a black person and the others are white. I feel that we are all human beings, and that's what I like.'

I then asked Paul for the pluses and minuses of life in Jersey. 'I think that life is good here. St Helier is so much safer than Nairobi. Here you can walk through the town at night. And another thing: working here, I have no need to take the bus; I can reach all parts of St Helier on foot and that's a big plus. I enjoy Jersey's countryside with the Jersey cow. I learned about Jersey cows at my Kenyan primary school but never dreamt that I would have the opportunity of seeing them in their birthplace. As to minuses, I miss the food at home. In Kenya we cook maize flour. And there's no goat on the menu in Jersey. Goat roasted on a barbecue; it's delicious!'

I came away from Norfolk Lodge conscious of the big contribution that Paul and his wife were making to the Island's tourist industry. Paul's last words to me were generous indeed: 'I express my appreciation to the Jersey people for allowing us to come over here.'

3

The Royal Square to Almorah Crescent by way of New Street, Union Street, Halkett Place, Val Plaisant and Midvale Road

At the western end of the Royal Square is a tall 18th century three-storey-and-attic stuccoed building, home since 1900 to the United Club. It originally contained an arcaded market-house on the ground floor but its granite arches have been lost ('cannibalised', says Brett) by the single storey extension that now houses Jersey's registry office. The first floor has tall French windows and it was in the handsome room behind them that I chatted to Colin Smith, the United Club's honorary secretary. I was very much in gentlemen's clubland: tables at one end invitingly laid up for lunch and at the other deep leather armchairs and a low table heaped with newspapers and magazines (including incidentally *Private Eye*). And one other thing about this fine room: the elderly John Wesley, on a visit to the Island in 1787, actually preached a sermon in it.

Suitably impressed, I turned to Colin and learned that he had been born in Hounslow, Middlesex, came to Jersey as a chartered quantity surveyor in 1960 intending to stay two years, married a local girl and has lived in the Island ever since, having retired in 2000 from his company, Colin Smith Partnership. Now the Club's secretary, he was its President from 2000 to 2003. He told me something of its history: 'The Club was founded in 1848 and met in various premises, probably pubs mostly, until moving here in 1900. We actually became owners of the property in 1932.'

I went on to ask Colin about the Club's membership. His reply to my first question was clear: 'Yes, we are gentlemen only and I hope that we shall always stay that way, purely for the tradition rather than anything else.' He laughed at a ribald remark from me and continued, 'No, we are certainly not misogynists. Ladies are allowed in after 5 p.m. and we have a number of functions to which partners are invited. As to membership numbers we have currently nearly 500 and that includes some who are overseas. We've capped the resident membership at

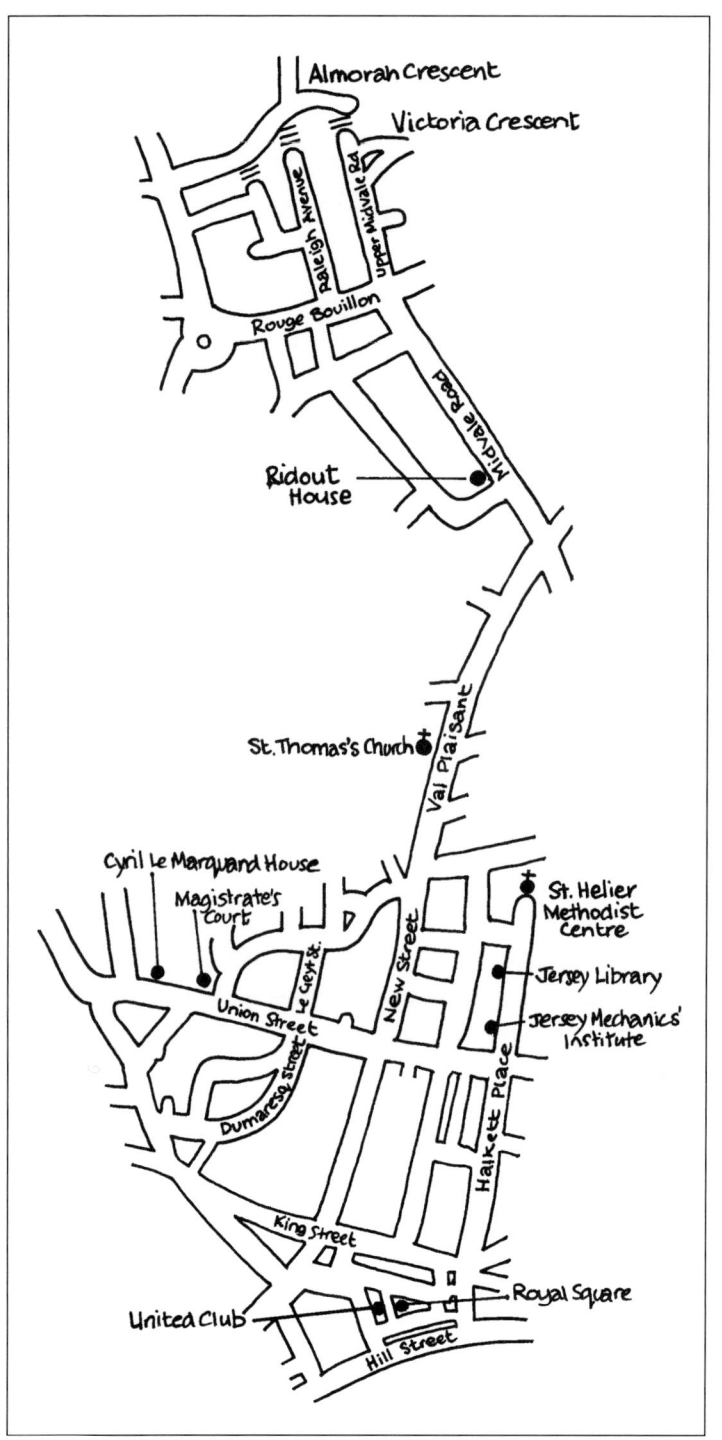

450. Lunchtime is our busiest period, and in the summer we open up the windows and use the balcony overlooking the Royal Square.'

Le Petit Greek Café, Royal Square

Now Colin and I were once together on the Council of the National Trust for Jersey, and he became its President for three years in 2005. His professional experience and qualifications surely made him an admirable choice and I turned our conversation to matters concerning the Island's heritage and architecture. He filled me in: 'The preservation of Jersey's countryside is a constant battle to prevent its erosion with the continual demand for more housing. It is so important that we don't lose that truly rural aspect of Jersey. Fly over Guernsey and you see that it is built up all over the place and spoiled; fly over Jersey and it remains quite green. That is what we have to fight for and defend.'

Two particular issues took up much of Colin's time and attention during his presidency. One concerned Plémont, the abandoned holiday camp and the future of this important headland. Colin's view on this is firm: 'It should be bought by the States in the long-term interests of the Island, and I think that there's a will among the politicians for this to come about.' The other matter was the National Trust's acquisition of No.16 New Street, gifted by the owners of de Gruchy's department store. I myself had been a member of the Council when the decision was taken to take up the challenge and restore this important 18th century townhouse and was interested to learn about its progress. Colin told me this: 'It is necessarily a slow job. That's the nature of the work. The faith of the Trust in taking it on has been and is fully justified. Not only is it saving a very important building but it will provide the Trust with a presence in St Helier which it has previously lacked.' These were words that I was much encouraged to hear as I took my leave of the United Club's committed secretary, made my way down King Street and turned in to New Street in order to see for myself how the work at No.16 was progressing.

~

Perhaps just a little history is needed. No.16 New Street was built around 1740 and is one of the finest remaining early Georgian houses in St Helier. It was extensively altered in the early part of the 19th century and thus its ground floor level, its front door, its façade and its roof date from the 1830s. It is in essence a building of that later period around the bones of a 1740s house, with important features such as the main staircase surviving from the original build. In the late 19th century it was a gentlemen's club; early in the 20th century it was taken over by the YMCA; later it became a de Gruchy store-cum-workshop and for a time its curtain makers' department; more recently it declined into a sad empty shadow of its former self, with water pouring through, rampant dry rot and pigeon infestation in the attics and upper floors. The man overseeing its restoration on behalf of Jersey's National Trust is Antony Gibb and he was there waiting for me on the first floor as I went through the front door and clambered up the as yet unrestored staircase.

Antony is a conservation consultant, also engaged by Jersey Heritage and involved previously in the work a few years back at Mont Orgueil. He began by telling me about his early association with this important house. 'Warwick Rodwell, architectural historian and archeologist, got to know the building some time ago. He produced an architectural appraisal, putting forward various options: going back to the 1740s original building, restoring it as found in its totally changed state or bringing it back to its dominant period which is the early 19th century. And this last is the option that the National Trust chose.'

I asked Antony what sort of challenge the commission had presented and he replied in these terms: 'It is one of the most interesting of buildings. This is not the refurbishment of a house for people to live in; it is a public building and the brief is therefore different. You don't for example have to put in bathrooms; you can put things back in a more pure way, minimising the introduction of modern features. When people walk in through the front door, they should get a sense of how the house was in around the 1820s.'

Was the Trust right to take this project on? Antony's response was unsurprisingly affirmative: 'This is the sort of building that might have been turned into offices; it would have been saved but it would also have been inaccessible to the public. Instead the National Trust will have a late Georgian complement to the Victorian townhouse museum in Pier Road and the public will have access and walk through rooms decorated in the style of the period, with furniture and paintings to match. There will be a National Trust shop on the ground floor and opportunities for rooms to be hired for a variety of social functions – dinners, meetings and so on.'

Antony then gave me a most comprehensive tour through all the rooms, pointing out at one stage a rudimentary system dating from the gentlemen's club era when holes were drilled in window frames and a ventilation shaft constructed through the roof, devices to remove the nicotine and smoke of the members' cigars. We then mounted the scaffolding on the outside and viewed the superbly restored roof and the outside walls ready for the stucco to be replaced.

At the back there is a new single-storey extension with modern facilities for the weddings, parties, conferences and events to which use No.16 in future will lend itself. And Antony had a final observation to make on this exciting project: 'After this historic house has been dark for so many years, passers-by will walk down New Street of an evening; the lights will be shining from the windows; it will be a welcoming sight with people streaming in and out. What a marvellous addition to the very heart of St Helier.'

~

Before I left 16 New Street I had a word with an old acquaintance, Ernie Le Brun, the National Trust's highly respected properties manager and originally a carpenter by trade. Ernie heads the Trust's in-house labour force undertaking the majority of the work here. He is still hands-on with the tools and told me something of the problems that the building has presented to him and his team. 'We're into our third year now. When we walked in the first time it revealed itself as a great challenge: the water was pouring in and when I walked through the front door I could see the sky. We used probably twice as much scaffolding inside as out, and we made a start cutting the rotting beams out, working from the top of the house downwards. It's all been something of a back-to-front job.' I asked Ernie whether it has been a satisfying project for him and his colleagues. He replied: 'It is the biggest job that we have ever undertaken. If a commercial builder had been put in, you would have had four walls and that would have been that, starting from the ground floor up. It has been much more complex than that. When it is finished it will be something for the Trust to boast about.' It was clear to me that Ernie Le Brun and his fellows were contributing enormous skill and expertise to this remarkable restoration. With a hailstorm raging outside I stepped out into the wet street, dampened but excited and content that the No.16 New Street project, with my small involvement some years before in the decision to take it on, was now moving towards its very satisfying completion.

~

Across the road from No.16 is St Paul's, according to Brett 'an unassuming and rather unexciting modest Gothic revival church of pink granite with grey granite dressings and a small bellcote'. Reasonably knowledgeable about religious matters, both interested and perhaps too full of doubt, I was tempted to make a visit and search out a member of the St Paul's congregation to tell me about its evangelical tradition and - a seeming consequence - its reputedly large Sunday attendances. I decided otherwise; there were yet more places of worship ahead on my journey round St Helier and I wished my account to be something rather more than a 'church crawl'. Instead I stepped out along New Street, turned left into Union Street and headed for the distinctive (a kind description) Cyril Le Marquand House. On my way I noticed Dumaresq Street off to the left and recalled that here were the offices of Tristan Lewis's Phoenix Trust & Company Software. I have known Tristan for some years; he is a member of my Oxford college and I gave him a small amount of help when for his degree in Politics, Philosophy and Economics he was writing a long essay on the Clothier Commission report into Jersey's machinery of government. I now wanted to learn what he had been up to during the intervening period. I made contact and he insisted on taking me to lunch at the Victoria Club in Beresford Street (certainly not a feature of this particular walk). Over good food and a glass of wine he reminded me of his past and brought me up to date.

Tristan's education was complicated by the fact that his father went to the United States in 1987 as a senior vice-president and chief financial officer of Duracell International. Tristan stayed in England and went to school at Winchester College (Manners Makyth Man and this was very much in evidence over the lunch table). After Pembroke, Oxford, he qualified as a chartered accountant with Deloitte in Jersey and then spent two years with Dominion Fiduciary Group. In 2006 he went into business with a couple of friends and became the managing director of Phoenix with the mission to grow its software package business.

I was more than usually in danger of being out of my depth and asked Tristan to explain simply what Phoenix Trust and Company Software was all about. He responded: 'Our business comes from selling software to trust companies, banks, accountancy practices, lawyers and so on, even other software companies. Take a trust company for example: an employee gets to work and fires up his or her computer; he will start Phoenix to run all his daily business. He will want to record some time for his time-sheet – Phoenix; there may be a new client and his details will be recorded on Phoenix; he wants to find compliance details – Phoenix; sending a bill, generating a work in progress report, getting management information for the MD to illustrate the company position, annual returns, share registers, anything that a trust company has to do – all this Phoenix will do. And its key benefits over other rival systems: it works and it's easy to use.' And what actually is it? I asked. 'A metaphorical box with a CD in it,' was the reply. 'Our business model goes thus: if you're selling rubbish or ripping people off, then you're dead. As it is, we are here for our clients and able to offer support and training. We charge a fee for annual maintenance and provide the help and advice that build up a strong and profitable relationship.'

Tristan told me more: the take-up in Jersey, Guernsey, the Cayman Islands, Switzerland, Nicosia and the UK and the employment of a local graphic design person to give the software product a new appearance and up-to-the-minute looks. He also described software developments concerning compliance – making sure that one's business is legal. 'What this means is the potential to come up with a product that forces employees to ensure that they are meeting all the regulations. There is business to be done and in six months we should be in the market-place with a development.'

I was wiser than I had been half an hour previously. With his considerable experience of Jersey's finance sector I wanted to learn Tristan's thoughts on its future prospects. He answered me in these terms: 'Five years ago all the talk was that Jersey finance was going down the tube. That has not happened and finance is booming. When people feel threatened as they do now, they want to put their money somewhere safe. Jersey is, I think, safer than other places. Fortunately none of our own clients has gone to the wall. So the message should perhaps be this: run Phoenix and you'll stay in business. I think that Jersey will be all right. Yes, it is difficult but I am an optimist. Of course I have a vested interest, but I hope that this is more than wishful thinking.'

Tristan Lewis has now been a Jersey resident for over a decade. What, I asked, were his more general thoughts about life in the Island? 'To be honest I have gone desperately native. When I first came to Jersey I was on the plane most weekends to get out and go to the UK, with friends telling me that I should come and live and work in London. Now fast-forward five years and these friends would do anything to move here. London life can be taxing; think of the Tube and the commute, the pollution and the gun crime. I would rather not be anywhere else but here. I don't like hustle and bustle; getting up at 5 in the morning and fighting through bad breath and body odour in the Underground are not for me. My friends come over here and after a few days say "I have washed my lungs". One changes one's outlook as one gets older, and when you run your own business your priorities alter massively. I do want to get on in business; this is a huge motivator for me. I am giving this business my best shot; I decided to go it alone and am having some fun along the way. So far it is paying off and I am content.'

And did Tristan, very much part of Jersey's financial scene, have a final thought? 'If they continue to buy Phoenix, then you and I will go out for lunch again. Perhaps I should take a full-page spread on the back cover of your book.'

~

It was time to resume my journey, return to Union Street and head for Cyril Le Marquand House. This high and unfortunate nine-storey States office block, named after the Senator whose policies over twenty-one years were to a large extent responsible for the growth of Jersey's finance industry, was opened in 1982 and is hardly St Helier's most handsome piece of architecture. Maurice Boots tells us that 'its superstructure is a reinforced concrete frame clad with smooth precast white wall slabs made from white calcinated flint obtainable in Normandy'. Its dominant and unprepossessing external appearance did not suggest what I was to experience as I entered and took the lift to the swish and smart modern suite of offices on the fourth floor that is the base of Jersey's Chief Minister and of his closest adviser, the man whom I had come to see, Bill Ogley, Chief Executive to the Council of Ministers.

Bill told me something of his early life and career: 'I was born in East Kent and went to school there and after that to Manchester University where I did a degree in Psychology and Physics. I then went on to qualify as an accountant. My two most recent jobs before coming to Jersey in 2003 were first in Whitehall as Deputy Controller of the Audit Commission and then nine years as Chief Executive of Hertfordshire County Council.' Was he, I asked, the nearest we have in Jersey to Cabinet Secretary Sir Humphrey Appleby? His reply was brisk: 'Yes, I am.' He added, 'Before ministerial government each department was an independent unit. Now I advise the Council of Ministers. I am the most senior manager in the States and responsible for all of the States' staff.'

My next question was a silly one: was ministerial government working well? I reframed it: how was ministerial government an improvement on the old committee system? Bill gave me a reassuring answer: 'Gone are the days when a committee would make a decision and another committee would consider it and criticise it. Now we have the ability to work across departments and what emerges is a synthesised view. Another advantage is this: we can now have an integrated management structure, introduce and manage programmes across the States, and this means integrated policies and efficiency savings. Also we can now act much more quickly than under the old committee system. And ministerial government has created a political nexus for relationships with other governments and countries, and that for example is better for our links with Whitehall and, for example, with France. These are essentially political in nature.'

JOURNEY ROUND St HELIER ~

I then bowled Bill Ogley a few googlies, all of which he faced up to with a confident straight bat. First I questioned him on the size of Jersey's public service: why not privatise some of it and put out more States work to tender? Bill's response was this: 'We have getting on for 7000 people employed by the States and this includes not only manual workers but also teachers, doctors, nurses, prison officers and so on. Compare us to European states and you will find that our public sector in percentage terms is considerably less. Use comparators and you will find that the number of our employees is low. We do in fact put out work to the private sector when it is a cheaper alternative; IT is a good instance of this. It is horses for courses. True, our manual workers are more highly paid than their private sector counterparts. If some of these jobs were outsourced, then there would be the tendency of boosting migration levels, bringing in people being paid at lower wage rates. Also if more work were put out to tender, then the effect on industrial relations would have to be considered and could be serious.' Did this mean that the TGWU had some sort of stranglehold? Bill's response to this was as follows: 'We have successfully confronted the manual workers on various occasions and been successful, but it has to be a softly, softly approach. We have done more than credit is given, and I would rather do it and be criticised for not doing it than have the airport closed. Remember the reality: if the harbour were closed, then within ten days the Island would have no food.'

My next bowl at the wicket concerned recent criticism from a newly elected States Member that Jersey's senior civil servants were both clever and empire-building while the politicians were less bright and hence lacking the capacity to keep them under control. Bill's answer to this was robust: 'Find me the evidence of empire-building. Go back again to the comparators with the UK, Guernsey, the Caymans and the Isle of Man and we come out very well. Study the report of the Comptroller and Auditor General and his findings that we have made all possible efficiency savings. The only remaining scope for further savings is to cut salary levels for the lower paid staff in every group; they are the ones who are relatively overpaid as compared with the UK. But I have to tell you that there is no political will to cut the pay of manual workers, junior civil servants, junior prison officers or the like. Your politician in the Saturday morning supermarket queue or walking down King Street would not have an easy time.'

My last ball was a tricky one: what about all the outside consultants? Why couldn't our civil servants do the job themselves? Bill's reply to this was as firm as his other answers: 'It depends how professional a job you want done. We don't have the expertise or the skills to do every high-level job ourselves. Take for example Transport and Technical Services where there is one person that deals with traffic and transport; if you want to look at the waterfront and consider putting a road underground with all the traffic flow consequences of the operation, then you sensibly bring in a UK professional who is dealing with such matters day in and day out. We don't employ consultants in order to avoid making difficult decisions ourselves; we bring them in for specialist assignments. In my department here I call them in for technical work in our IT section for the simple reason that we don't employ web-based programmers whose services would only be needed occasionally. It was also right for example to bring in a media consultant at the height of the Haut de la Garenne saga; we did not have the expertise to deal with the massive national media attention. It comes down to this: does Jersey want high quality government that the Island expects or is it a matter of make do and mend?'

Bill Ogley had surely scored well; my bowling average was poor. I turned to somewhat easier matters in asking our chief civil servant, who before his arrival in 2003 had never before been to Jersey, how he would sum up his views on the nature of his and his family's new home. 'Jersey is totally unlike anywhere else. Its virtues are many: the environment of course, but the closeness, the politeness, the sense of community and its safety. In the UK you are faceless and unknown; in Jersey we live in an open and safe society. Our population is near 90,000, but the range of facilities is exceptional. Such quality and such opportunities to experience in this relatively small island!'

What then, I asked, were the drawbacks? 'We have to be mindful of the circumstances of how certain parts of our community live. This is primarily related to non-qualified housing and the issues of overcrowding and difficult living conditions. It is a major social problem that has to be addressed. But despite that, Jersey is overall a much more integrated community than in the UK where multiculturalism has in places created a fractured society. Here we are all part of the same community, but we must work towards those on lower incomes and without housing qualifications being better integrated into an Island that has so much to offer.'

~

Next door to Cyril Le Marquand House is a handsome and very modern building opened by the Bailiff in 2006. A piece of polished marble outside explains its function – The Magistrate's Court. (Yes, Lynne Truss can relax. This is not the greengrocers' apostrophe; there may be assistant and relief magistrates, but there is only one magistrate.) I walked into the very smart reception area and was given a warm welcome by the court greffier, David Le Heuzé. It was a Friday afternoon; none of the three courts was being used; and before I sat down and asked David a few questions he gave me a most comprehensive tour of his new domain, telling me first about the building itself. 'The project for a new magistrate's court is in fact a very old one, first mooted in 1967. Our previous Dickensian set-up was neither adequate nor human rights compliant, and the States architects have done a magnificent job (and the probation service also has its purpose-built offices here). A number of factors were involved in the design: the totally secure environment that the police require, a completely open environment to satisfy the advocates, and consideration for litigants in the petty debts court. It was a challenge and it was achieved.'

Magistrate's Court

David then led me on an extensive tour. We first went into the open court with its modern layout, its widened aisles for the disabled, its sophisticated CCTV, its disguised hearing loops and its state-of-the-art air conditioning (air replacement rather than forced air so that the room has the quiet of a library). We then moved to the custody suite and its secure interview rooms, its cells (only occasionally have they been used overnight during a police emergency) and outside yard with its three electrically interlocked doors (allowing only one open at a time). Next was Court 1, the fully secure court, with its arrangements to protect the court officers from the defendant (and even, if needed, from members of the public), as well as protecting the defendant from the public, separated by a glass screen capable of stopping a 9mm bullet. Lastly there was the semi-secure court, the one most in use. David and I stood behind the bench and he made clear his admiration for the magistrates presiding over the court – for them what could be a relatively intimidating experience with the whole room hanging on every one of their words.

Finally we came to a small library. We sat down and I was able to find out a little more about my personable guide. David Le Heuzé told me this: 'No, I'm not a lawyer. Actually I joined the RAF when I was fifteen and a half as a technician and was later commissioned into the education branch. I took voluntary redundancy in 1997 and this post came up in 2001, with its big challenge to plan and oversee the establishment of the new Magistrate's Court.'

David explained how the court works: 'Besides the magistrate we have an assistant magistrate and several relief magistrates called in on an ad hoc basis. Yes, it has always in living memory been a stipendiary system, although the first magistrate was a Jurat, and Jurats can still technically sit. The magistrate's court sits every morning, the petty debts court on a Wednesday and the youth court on Tuesday mornings and afternoons. And the Royal Court sits here occasionally when there is a security aspect to the case. Indeed judicial history was made a year ago when at the same time and in this one building we had sitting the Royal Court, the Magistrate's Court and the Appeal Court.'

David answered my queries about committal proceedings, with criminal cases normally coming first to the Magistrate's Court but with the Attorney General having the right to indict direct to the Royal Court. And I also learned how much this impressive new building was being used. 'The footfall here,' he told me, 'must be in excess of 25,000 a year. On average we deal with 3,500 cases in the criminal court each year, and there are 8,000 or so civil cases.' I could only think that the whole operation must run smoothly indeed in these most modern premises. I said my farewells to David, glad to have seen the Magistrate's Court as an interested spectator rather than as a defendant. I resolved to keep my speed below 40 mph on Victoria Avenue and more often to take a taxi when eating out.

~

The 1960s saw large areas of Town, in particular the environs of Union Street, redeveloped with high-rise blocks of flats such as Hue Court constructed at the cost of many 18th and 19th century buildings, demolished to make room for these now out-of-fashion intrusions. Almost opposite Hue Court is Le Geyt Street and a few yards along it is a shop called Polskie Delicateski. One does not require a detailed knowledge of Polish in order to see that this is a food shop for some of Jersey's most recent and fairly prolific immigrants. I entered and had a chat with

Anna Brzozowski who was serving behind the counter.

Anna, with perfect English learned at a summer language school in Eastbourne, came to Jersey in 2002, getting employment through a Warsaw job centre at the then Silver Springs Hotel in St Brelade. How long, I asked her, had the shop been functioning? She replied: 'Two years. Some Jersey people come in and are tempted by our Polish food. The problem is that they are sometimes afraid to ask what this or that is. And when I am busy I do not have the time to explain.' I then asked Anna to tell me more about the Polish community in the Island. She answered in this way: 'When I arrived in Jersey there were perhaps 800 to 900 Poles; now in the summer season there are several thousand. But many are now leaving: there is the pound against the euro and a somewhat improved economic situation in Poland, and this makes employment in Jersey less attractive. Also we now have to pay tax on our salaries and that, combined with high accommodation costs, is another factor making the Island less of a good employment prospect.' I then asked Anna whether the Poles tended to stick closely together similarly to many in Jersey's Portuguese community. Her response suggested that the two communities and their relationship with Jersey were somewhat different: 'Polish people are quite open. They share the same sense of humour as Jersey and English people. There's the same sense of freedom and fun. And you have probably noticed that Polish people work hard and work long. They're always prepared to stay on and get a job done.' Anna then returned to her earlier topic: 'The numbers of Poles in Jersey are probably going to get less. It's the high cost of living, the income tax business and GST. It is getting a bit harder for us.'

~

I left Anna and her well-stocked and orderly Polskie Delicateski and walked back to Union Street, continuing along Burrard Street and turning left into Halkett Place. At once on the left was the Jersey Mechanics' Institute, built in 1873 as Albert Hall and serving as the Post Office from 1881 to 1909. It has a remarkable façade which those going to the Jersey Library next door or the Methodist Centre at the end of the road can hardly miss. Brett deserves to be fully quoted here: 'An ornate building in a sort of baroque style, very tall…with much polychrome ornament applied in stucco above the windows and the oculus window in the attic parapet. The decorative themes include oak leaves and acorns and exotic fruits, with on the ground floor female masks and above the central round-headed window a male bearded mask, all richly coloured and gilded…' Brett, writing in 1977, also points out that the overall splendid effect is just a little spoiled by the unhappy siting of a parking sign up against the building. The sign remains in place more than thirty years later.

I made my way inside this surprising and unusual addition to the St Helier street scene, entered what seemed to be a large bar and met up with James Garvie, the Institute's steward. Better known as Jim, he came from Glasgow to Jersey in 1999, worked first at the Rozel Bay Hotel and then on a building site before being appointed to his current job in October, 2007. He explained to me what actually happens in the building: 'Downstairs here is the United Services Club. It's a social club. Upstairs is the Jersey Mechanics' Institute which is a snooker club with a membership of over 200 and another bar. Downstairs is essentially a working men's club where the alcohol is drunk; upstairs is busiest in the evenings and soft drinks are the order of the day.'

With Jim I climbed the stairs to his other responsibility (he is employed by the Mechanics' Institute but oversees the club downstairs as well) and found myself in a very large and tall panelled hall. Its size can be judged by the fact that it accommodates five full-size snooker tables, with room to spare, and three more on a higher mezzanine floor. This must surely be one of the largest rooms in St Helier and possibly one of the least known.

As I took all this in, Jim told me something about himself: 'I love Jersey. It has changed my life. I was out of work for seven years in Glasgow – partly my own fault – and a friend came over to the Island as a chef and invited me to come over too. What do I like about it here? Its atmosphere of friendliness. Like so many Glaswegians my mother and father used to come over on holiday in the 1950s and `60s when tourism was booming. And the Scots links with Jersey, dating from that time, remain strong.' And Jim's duties? He replied: 'I do twenty-eight hours behind the bars and the rest of my working time is occupied with the wages and the paperwork, organising the staff and the rotas, doing the tills and the finances of the club. I am loving every minute of it. I couldn't have asked for a better job at my time of life. I'm fifty-nine and hope to go on here to seventy.' I said goodbye to this contented fellow and walked next door to Jersey Library.

~

Jersey's first public library was founded by the Reverend Philip Falle and opened in 1743. In 1886 it moved to rooms in the States Building and there it remained in increasingly inadequate premises until it transferred in 1989 to new and spacious accommodation, opened on 25 May of that year by the Queen. As I stepped into this fine and airy modern building, cleverly designed so that its exterior relates to the Jersey Mechanics' Institute next door, I guessed that Jersey was more fortunate than most places in the United Kingdom where an increasing squeeze on local government finances over the years has made library provision a pale shadow of what was previously provided. My sense that this was so was strengthened by my meeting with Chief Librarian Pat Davis and the very comprehensive tour she gave me of this impressive educational and leisure facility. We started at the top of the building in the school resources department and then looked down from high up – it is an impressive atrium design - on the two floors below, with the big reference section, the local studies room and the main adult lending areas. I also looked into the quiet and air-controlled Falle Room where the founder's own library of 2,000 volumes is kept. Pat was able to give me some remarkable statistics: 459,408 items borrowed in 2007; 1,200 library visitors on average per day; 14,000 the average number of new items added each year; and a total stock of 183,000.

Before moving on, I caught up with a couple of people quietly reading and studying in the reference library. William Philpott had books and notes in front of him and told me that he was preparing a talk for his religious house group that night. 'Yes,' he told me, 'I worship at St Paul's. And we are studying a section of Mark's gospel. I'm a big library user, and the non-fiction downstairs particularly draws me.' At another desk was Gary Bisson who told me this: 'I use the library about twice a week. I'm doing an Open University degree in music; 20th century classical music – Stravinsky and so on. I have had recent experience of the library in Lincoln. It's not nearly as well stocked as this one.' I came down to the ground floor and bumped into an acquaintance, Sheelah Langlois, who described herself as an avid reader and very frequent user of the Library. With a degree from University College, London, and a former career teaching English at Beaulieu, this is unsurprising. She told me something of the Library's facilities: 'One of the big things is that it is free. I get out story cassettes which I play in the car; I use the reference section every so often; I usually have a couple of books out at any one time – modern fiction, the classics and so on. At present I'm re-reading Aldous Huxley's *Brave New World*. And I take the grandchildren there as well.' Sheelah must surely be one of Jersey Library's keenest borrowers.

As a past Librarian of The King's School, Canterbury, and as headmaster of two schools where I was able to rebuild and rehouse their library facilities, I was in my element (some boys wanted to be train drivers; I was always more interested in books and libraries). How fortunate Jersey is to have this marvellous Halkett Place library, well staffed and well stocked and seemingly a haven for students and book-lovers of all ages.

~

At the end of Halkett Place is St Helier Methodist Centre. Now it has to be said that there is something slightly unsatisfactory about its position and appearance since its frontage is too broad for the comparatively narrow street on the axis of which it stands. Brett is worth quoting here: 'An important building, closing the long vista up Halkett Place, stucco…In principle Italianate-classical, but an endearingly naïve piece of work…But this bastard-classical style makes a robust and useful contribution to any townscape'. It was built in 1847 and originally

Wesley Grove

known as Grove Place. Years later it combined with Wesley Chapel and became Wesley Grove; and only a few years ago, around the time of a major restoration in 2000, Aquila Road Methodist church amalgamated with it, and hence the new name of St Helier Methodist Centre. In the very modern ancillary buildings is the office of its minister, the Reverend Liz Hunter, and I called on her there.

Liz describes herself as a Devonian through and through, grew up in Newton Abbot and on leaving school joined the Royal Air Force, spending eight years as an air traffic control officer. She told me that there was no Damascus Road experience bringing her to the ministry: 'When my elder daughter was born I started asking myself the questions that she would one day ask me. That challenged my faith and my thinking. I had the grounding of childhood Methodist Sunday school and teenage church youth club. I started returning to church and everything developed from there. I was ordained in 2003 and came to Jersey in 2004. This is my first full-time appointment in the ministry.'

Liz Hunter went on to describe to me the system by which Methodist appointments are made: 'It's a cross between *Blind Date* and the draw for the FA Cup, but it is actually a prayerful procedure and rarely comes up with the wrong answer.' She also told me about some of the various activities at the Centre besides the Sunday worship: 'There is a mother and toddler group, the Friday soup and bread lunches, the day-care nursery which is open five days a week with its forty-seven children, and Alcoholics Anonymous also meets here twice a week.'

Over the years I have attended concerts in the church itself, with its large and impressive interior, its gallery carried on cast-iron columns and a handsome organ case in the recess behind a particularly large prayer desk-cum-pulpit. What was the size of Sunday congregations for this spacious church? 'We have between fifty and a hundred depending on various factors – time of year, holiday periods, even the state of the weather. It's a good cross-section of people. We have video projectors and an excellent sound system and we try to encourage our youngsters to be involved in the music and drama. Numbers are on a plateau, but it is true that membership is, as with other denominations, decreasing.'

Liz went on to tell me about some of the social problems which she encounters. 'There are the youngsters and the youths who at times hang around on the steps outside. We also have a good working relationship with Citizens' Advice Bureau for those needing financial assistance. People with problems sometimes come to our Friday lunches. And we have a community coffee bar on Monday and Wednesday mornings where there's always somebody here as a listening ear.'

Always interested in how those new to the Island take to it, I finally quizzed Liz Hunter about herself and Jersey? 'I absolutely love it and for many reasons. Everybody seems to know everybody else. Whatever people say about society no longer being what it once was, there is this great community sense, an interconnection that makes it a special place. There's the scenery of course; where else could I be a Methodist minister and drive round almost any corner and see the sea? I was brought up close to the sea and this is important to me. Yes, there are problems. There are drugs and drink but, I guess, no greater a problem than anywhere else. There is the finance industry and an emphasis on material goods: that for me as a Christian is an issue to be noted and wrestled with. But on balance Jersey is such a generous place with a huge response to people in need and so much charitable work.' And a final thought from the Methodist Centre's active and committed minister? 'What lies behind these blue steps and blue doors at the top of Halkett Place is a warm welcome and a great deal of regard and love for the Island community.'

~

My way ahead was round the side of the Methodist Centre, into Vauxhall Street and then left towards Val Plaisant. My intention had been to slip a few yards down New Street and call at the district office of Unite, the successor of the Transport and General Workers' Union. Its Regional Industrial Officer, with a large membership among the States workforce, is Nick Corbel. But my various efforts to meet him were frustrated: my initial letter plus phone call and a subsequent personal visit when I encountered him at the other side of the reception desk had elicited the promise of a few minutes of his precious time. Mr Corbel failed to get in touch. A further letter when I suggested that I wanted the Union answers to some of the questions previously put to Bill Ogley, Chief Executive of the States, also did not produce a response. I gave up.

Instead I moved north up Val Plaisant, with St Thomas's Roman Catholic church and its tall, thin spire coming into view. It was opened in 1883 and built for French Roman Catholics (the Anglo-Irish community had its own church round the corner in Vauxhall Street) and indeed its detail is French and its size that of a small cathedral. It has recently undergone major renovation and its interior is perhaps more impressive than its exterior. I am particularly acquainted with its high west end organ gallery; it is better if one does not suffer from vertigo when playing for services here. Next door to the church is the Presbytery and I rang the bell in order to have a chat with Monsignor Nicholas France, Jersey's Catholic Dean.

Father France first told me something of his early life: born in Sussex and educated at Douai, the Benedictine boarding school. He studied for the priesthood at the Westminster Seminary and was ordained in 1968. As chaplain to Bishop Worlock of Portsmouth (later Archbishop of Liverpool), he made frequent visits to Jersey. He was Catholic Dean of Southampton before taking up his current responsibilities in the Island in 1999, being, as he told me, 'the first non-French priest at St Thomas's in spite of my bearing the surname France.'

I asked about his early background – father an agnostic Anglican and mother a Catholic – and whether he had had some sort of Damascus Road conversion experience. 'No,' replied Nicholas France, ' I am more like Peter than Paul: stop-start all along the way; a long slog; making mistakes, picking oneself up and moving on. There was once a novice who went to the Abbot of Downside and said, "Father Abbot, I have been seeing visions." The abbot replied, "We just don't do this sort of thing, Brother, in the English Benedictines."'

Father France and I then discussed St Thomas's and its recent restoration. 'Yes, I am very heartened and pleased by the results. We have moved away from the rather puritanical 1970s. For example we've created a French shrine to Our Lady of Lourdes. There's a memorial to Francois Scornet, the youth shot by the Germans at St Ouen's Manor during the Occupation. A dull doorway has been turned into a beautiful shrine for Our Lady of Czestochowa, the Queen of Poland. Another chapel has painted tiles portraying the scene of Fatima; hence the Portuguese have a little of Portugal here. We have tried to celebrate all our different cultures and enrich the place with beauty. God is beauty; if we can touch beauty in different ways – music, architecture, art – then the spirit is lifted.'

Monsignor France has brought the two parishes of St Thomas and of St Mary and St Peter together. He continued, 'Today the Island's Catholic church serves what are essentially several communities – Jersey, Portuguese, Polish and not insignificant numbers of Scots, Irish and, increasingly, Filipinos working for the likes of PricewaterhouseCoopers. We had 1,400 at Mass last Sunday in St Helier. It's hard work and we have too few priests. I find it especially difficult to attract a Portuguese priest to the Island. I am getting older; I have been forty years a priest and the work does not get less.'

Nicholas France now told me what else had happened on the site. 'This is terribly important. To me one of the greatest achievements has not been the restoration of St Thomas's but the establishment of our Welcome Centre in the old school buildings. When I came here these were derelict. With much fund-raising and great help from Dick Shenton and Lieutenant Governor Sir John Cheshire we converted them into a place where, besides rooms with other functions, Highlands College provides the teachers and we the ambience and support system that has allowed a total of over 3,000 people to come here to learn English. To me this is the best thing that I could have done for Jersey, empowering what is something of a fractured society with language. The problem otherwise is this: the Portuguese are invisible; you don't notice them; they do the work; they have left home and are spiritually impoverished. The Welcome Centre has allowed us to address some of these issues.'

I now lobbed a few possibly tricky questions in Father France's direction, my first being this: was he himself a liberal Catholic? There was a slight pause and this was his answer: 'Not really. I am middle of the road. You see it is not my church.

People ask me what my view on this or that is. I say to them that I have got no views; I have the teaching of the Church; it is what the Church teaches that I believe.' I then asked him how he equated an excellent relationship with the Anglican Dean and other non-Catholic clergy when the Catholic church did not recognise their orders as being valid. He replied: 'This question was asked of Archbishop Worlock in regard to his close friendship with Bishop David Sheppard in Liverpool. His answer was along these lines: "We respect you as a valid bishop of the Church of England if not of our Church."'

What about contraception and the Catholic teaching contained in *Humanae Vitae*? 'A difficult matter,' Monsignor France replied. 'It is a high ideal to aim at though people have to follow their conscience on this one if their situation is itself not "ideal". It is a bit like Jesus saying "Love your enemy"; but let's try and love our neighbour first. Most Catholics have made up their own minds on this one.' Women priests? Married priests? 'Not likely. Indeed a sad thing of my life has been the failure of union with the Anglicans. The women priest issue has meant that we are now much further apart.'

We ended our chat with the Catholic Dean telling me about the social problems that are very close to home in this part of Town. 'I have never experienced such drug problems as I do here: drug deals behind the church; needles in the forecourt. I have parishioners in prison; youths in prison with HIV. Yes, it is a church for sinners. And what are the causes? It is partly the 'haves' and 'have nots' divisions in Jersey. There are so many social problems – the break-up of families, multiple occupancy, Poles living many to a room. I can go from a visit to a millionaire's house to see people living in one room, mother and daughter sharing the same bed, and round the walls a TV, a basin, a fridge and a little cooker, with the loo downstairs and shared with others.'

Monsignor France movingly summed this all up: 'One goes from one thing to another. I enjoy it; and at least I am here and should be here. When they say that St Thomas's is in a seedy part of Town, I say "Thank God". That's where it should be.'

~

Before moving on up Val Plaisant I popped into the church itself, once again admiring its cathedral-like dimensions and the improvements wrought by its recent restoration. I was fortunate in being able to have a word with Nancy Murphy, a member of the Guild of St Thomas, sitting at the back and doing her stint as guide and guardian of this special place. She told me that the church is open from 9 a.m. till 6 p.m., with people dropping in for prayer and quietness and lighting a candle. She also told me that her family, with its Irish name and connections, had belonged to the Irish church, St Mary and St Peter, and she added this: 'I was born in Jersey just before the war. When the old church in Vauxhall Street was demolished, that was a real break with the past. We then came regularly here to St Thomas's and I had a great fondness for the French priests. That was when I was eight or nine. One Sunday a month was Men's Sunday when the whole of the main aisles were filled with men. There was a special sermon for them and the singing was exceptional.'

Nancy Murphy continued: 'I don't remember much about the Occupation but I understand that the German soldiers came here then. So we had this extraordinary situation: the Germans in the middle and the parishioners down the side aisles, all praying to the same God and hoping that their side would win the war.' And the recent restoration? 'We owe a great debt of gratitude to Monsignor France and of course to Daphne Minihane who played such a large part in fund-raising. And we have the central aisle restored now; I think of all those brides in the past who had to process up the side. The new arrangement lends itself perfectly to fine ceremonial.'

I left our dedicated guardian at her desk near the back, walked out into Val Plaisant and turned left towards Midvale Road.

~

Midvale Road is architecturally special: a street of fine stucco late-Regency-style terraces and villas. One of the first of these handsome buildings on the left is Ridout House, a home where for a number of years my sister-in-law, the late Louise Williams, had chaired its committee and where its mission is, in the words of its brochure, 'to provide for elderly Jersey residents an affordable community home with emphasis placed on informality and a happy atmosphere throughout'. Its origins are interesting: in 1970 a group of ladies, led by the redoubtable Betty Le Brocq, formed a discussion group to investigate the possibilities of housing on a permanent basis those persons who lived in Jersey's hotels during the winter months and then had to find alternative accommodation during the summer tourist season. In due course Windsor House round the corner in Val Plaisant was acquired for this purpose, and in 1993 the home transferred to its current premises, having been left the property in the will of its owner, Mrs Ridout. I rang the bell and was warmly welcomed by the Head of House, Norma Parkinson. She took me into the home's sitting room, with its big windows and fine view over a lovely garden at the back, and told me about herself and her work.

Norma first came to Jersey in 1985, caring for old people. She was invited to take up the post of live-in manager at Windsor House and told me of her enthusiasm in accepting the invitation: 'The idea appealed to me. It was a small care home; I could be involved and not sit in an office all day. It's very informal here – not institutionalised at all. And that was in 1989 and I have been Head of House ever since.' Norma went on to tell me more: a total of nine residents, with those paying who are able to, and the parish providing for the others. 'We are probably the least expensive home in the Island. All our residents have their own rooms which they furnish themselves and all with en-suite bathrooms. The transition here is easy for them; they can wake up in the morning and everything around them is their own.' There are eight staff in all, and Norma shares her basement flat with a huge hairy German shepherd dog (and a cat) which was out at the back and greeted by us through the windows. I learned of the fund-raising that goes to support Ridout House; and three years before, the Itex round-the-Island walk had donated some of its money towards a big refurbishment. Norma herself did twenty-six miles on that occasion with her Alsatian ('and I only bought the trainers three days before the event').

By this time the Head of House and I had been joined in the sitting room by Mrs Hales-Coleman who was proud to tell me that she had been a resident for twenty-eight years. She added this: 'I am nearly ninety-two, was born in India and educated in England. My children are in England and they come over and see me, and I get a letter almost daily.' I suggested to Mrs Hales-Coleman that she deserved a long service and good conduct medal. She replied: 'I am very happy here; it's the best place in the Island. The people are so kind and look after us so well. You don't have to move a finger'. At this point Norma interjected, 'The cheque will be in the post, Mrs Coleman.'

I was then given a tour of this happy and caring place and almost felt inclined to book my room as I said goodbye to Norma Parkinson and her enthusiastic staff.

~

High above St Helier are two remarkable 19th century architectural gems – Almorah Crescent started in 1844 and, below it, Victoria Crescent built ten years later. How many Island residents are aware of them? They are not greatly visible as one crosses Rouge Bouillon and climbs up Upper Midvale Road. Victoria Crescent, writes Brett, consists of 'seven pairs of fine tall three-storey houses, each connected to the next by a lower linking block; pilasters to each house; inset half-round columns flanking recessed panels in the top floor; mostly Georgian-glazed; placed on the hillside so as to look out over a semicircular field, planted with good trees, across the town'. Someone who knows much about Victoria Crescent is Bernard Morris, a former Victoria College pupil who went on to Queen's University, Belfast, later taking a diploma in planning at Kingston Polytechnic, working in various London boroughs, coming back to Jersey in 1973 as a planning officer with that States department and retiring in 1992. Bernard has the closest family connections with Victoria Crescent and I went to see him in order to find out more.

Victoria Crescent

How, I asked, had this fine terrace come into his family? He replied: 'Thomas Falle, the developer, went bust, and one of my forebears bought it as bankrupt stock along with other property in the area. Eventually it came into the possession of my mother and uncle, and that's how it came down to me.' I then asked Bernard to comment on the crescent's architecture. 'It is a very good example of Victorian planning,' he answered. 'You have the buildings set back and this green lung, parkland really, in front. It was part of the big mid-19th century developments in the north of St Helier, built in large measure for retirees and ex-army colonels. And it's typical of the upstairs/downstairs arrangement of the day – servants working in the basements and living in the attics. Indeed some of the houses had their old wired bell systems until quite recently. And Victoria Crescent differs from Almorah Crescent above: the former has split, semi-detached houses, and some might say that it is not quite as attractive as the latter with its continuous sweep. On the other hand you could argue that Almorah is somewhat more plain.'

Bernard continued: 'When my mother and uncle inherited, the crescent was in a bad state of repair, with the wooden shutters rotten, the road full of potholes and the little park in front hardly more than a dump. In the 1940s and '50s this was regarded almost as a twilight area of Town. Steadily improvements were made and, as properties became vacant, rewiring was undertaken and central heating and modern bathrooms were put in.'

Town planner Bernard and I then had a gossip about other aspects of St Helier's architectural heritage. We reflected on its fine Victorian buildings – the areas round Stopford Road, David Place and St Mark's Road – with so many villas now divided up and in the past badly treated (big lumpy dormer windows stuck into the roofs, for example) but slowly being restored and improved. Bernard was also interesting on the town's high-rise developments: 'High-rise came into fashion in 1960s England. A few years later it arrived here in Jersey – Convent Court near St Thomas's for instance. These developments were pushed by the States architects as a new way of living. Yes, they were based on the ideas of Le Corbusier, but only after the Ronan Point collapse in the UK did they go out of fashion. Then there's the Esplanade – something of a disaster. It is a muddle, and the problem there is that these were warehouses, stretching back to Commercial Street. So when redevelopment happens, you have long buildings with insufficient light coming in.'

Bernard had retired from the planning department before the Waterfront developments. He considers the flats as being reasonably adventurous for Jersey and dismissed Cineworld as just a lot of sheds that could easily be knocked down in the future. And the Hopkins plan for a finance centre? 'It is a huge development that could easily go wrong; and tunnelling the road below sea level could be a problem.' We had chatted enough and it was time for me to take my leave and climb higher to Almorah Crescent.

~

Why Almorah? The construction of this fine terrace was started in 1844 by Charles La Cloche Ricard, a speculative builder, and was named after his wife, born at Almorah in the Himalayas. Both Brett and Boots wax lyrical about it. Here is Brett: 'A splendid very tall crescent, on top of a steep hill, of ten white-painted stucco houses, each of two bays and four storeys…The ground floors very plain, rusticated…At the first floor, balconies topped by curving lead Regency canopies carried on slim black-painted wooden struts with cast-iron railings; shutters to the French windows on this floor. The Georgian-glazed windows on the floor above are inset in curved recesses with charming Regency canopies above…This is a splendid composition on a magnificent site'. Boots goes further: 'This splendid terrace is probably the finest, not only in Jersey, but also the finest amongst the south coast of England's examples'. Praise indeed!

Almorah Crescent

The western end of the terrace is occupied by the Almorah Hotel (with current proposals for conversion into flats) and standing outside its door as I approached was Alex Bosnovic who had recently taken up his post as manager. He gave me the green light to wander through its rooms and up to its top floor, with me taking my fill from the windows of panoramic views over St Helier below and the more distant sea. We then sat down in the hotel lounge, and Alex told me something about himself: originally from Czechoslovakia - Prague in fact - and twenty years in Florida and five in Brighton managing hotels before coming to Jersey in 2008. I asked him for his impressions of this remarkable terrace where his responsibilities now lay. He was admiring and enthusiastic: 'It is beautiful. Indeed the whole of Jersey is beautiful. When I moved to the UK I did not know where the Channel Islands were. The internet didn't help me: it turned up several channel islands off both Alaska and New Zealand. Eventually I booked my flight and arrived. I fell in love with Jersey at first sight.' I mentioned to Alex that I had visited Prague and said that we did not have Prague Castle to boast about. He would have none of this and retorted, 'But you have a nice castle too. What's wrong with Mont Orgueil?' To that I had no answer. I said goodbye, took a last look at what must surely be one of the finest pieces of Jersey architecture and made my way down the hill and back to the centre of St Helier.

4

The Royal Square to Windsor Crescent by way of the Market, David Place and Stopford Road

For my fourth journey it was time for me to head towards what many would consider the jewel in St Helier's crown – the Central Market – and I left the Royal Square, taking time to admire the late 17th century building on the north side that includes No.16, Gallichan the Jewellers, with its impressive shop front. Opposite Gallican's is The Peirson, aptly named and one of the Royal Square's two popular hostelries. On its wall is an interesting plaque:

> **Battle of Jersey**
> **January 6th 1781**
>
> At the time of the battle this building was the house of Dr Phillipe Lerrier. Major Peirson was killed near the corner of the house facing the market-place and Baron de Rullecourt died of his wounds inside the house. The patches on the wall above cover the marks made by bullets fired during the battle.

After this brief brush with history I left the square and made for the Halkett Place entrance to the Market and, not for the first time, marvelled at this fine structure built in 1882. Its outer casing is of dressed granite, with thirteen bays onto Halkett Place and ten on to Beresford Street. There is so much to impress, not least its airy internal dimensions and the glazed roof carried on ranges of cast-iron columns and floral metal struts. Brett considers the Market's octagonal central area as being reminiscent of the dome of a palm-house and rightly enthuses about the circular pool and fountain, with its goldfish-inhabited depths embracing an island of rockery and greenery. Brett says it all: 'A splendid and most satisfying centrepiece'. Boots adds his voice to the praise, stating that the object of the designer was to preserve the effect of what was originally an open market; hence

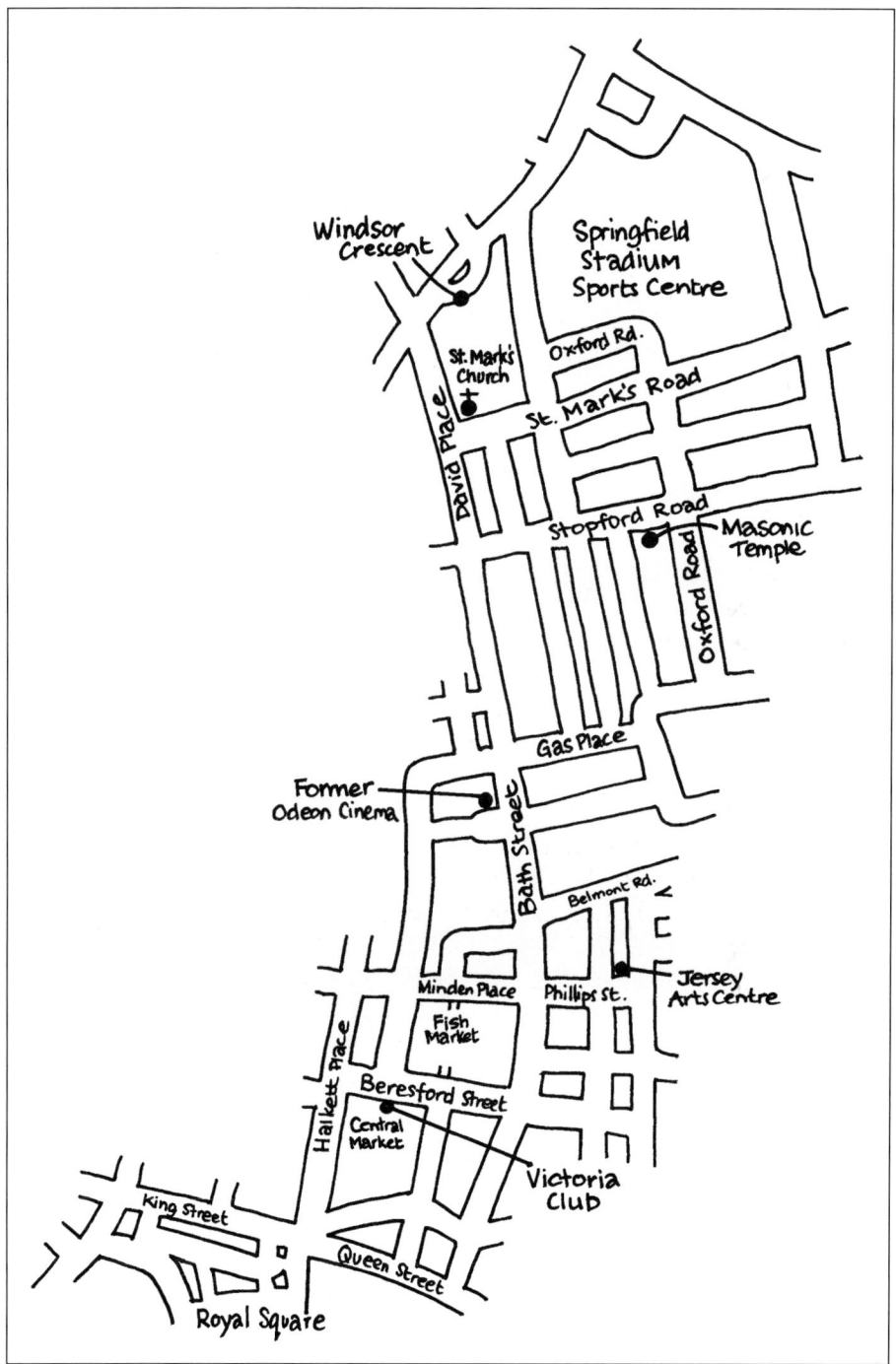

Market fountain

the resultant feeling of space with the dramatic quality of the glazing.

I wanted to have a chat with some of the Market's stallholders, but first I made my way past what may be the oldest pillar box in the British Isles – it certainly looked older than any I have ever previously seen – and climbed the stairs to the office of Greg Collenette who has been Market Inspector since 1991. Greg was educated at Hautlieu School and worked for seventeen years at Romeril's before taking up his present position, a States post, in charge of both the Central and the Fish Markets. What, I asked, was his job? He replied: 'I try to run the place with its forty-seven individual traders in the two markets. There are two distinct trades under the one roof – not only the fresh produce trades but also the closed shop trades such as the jewellers. It's quite a job trying to get agreement on opening hours that please them all. And they all pay rents with nine-year leases.'

Did Greg have a special affection for his domain? 'Well, I worked here at a greengrocer's after school, on Saturdays and in school holidays, and my mother worked here too. The Market and I go back quite a long way. As to the structure, it's sound and we're spending money on reglazing this year. The woodwork is all right and the ironwork okay.' Was there not a problem with the fountain some time ago? I asked. 'Yes,' replied Greg, 'that was very controversial; a bit of a nightmare. There was sort of volcanic rock incorporated in it, and the powers that be removed it. The heritage people were concerned and some of the replacement granite had to be taken back out.'

And what about the Market's viability in this day and age? Greg was optimistic: 'I would like to think that the Market will flourish. There is demand for the stalls when they become available; I haven't got tenants banging on my door and saying that they are selling up. So fingers crossed.' And were there any special problems with the Fish Market across the road? Greg gave me a surprising reply: 'Not really. We do sometimes get the shanky (brown) crabs crawling out of their baskets, and they have a habit of going down the pipes. And you cannot move them.'

My last question to the Market Inspector was about support from the politicians for this impressive States property. Greg Collenette gave me a suitably diplomatic 'Yes' in reply and told me that money was being spent on it after years of neglect. Having received from him some recommendations concerning stallholders who might be willing to chat with me, I thought it best to leave things there, thanked him and took my leave.

~

From Greg Collenette's office I walked across to the other side of the Market and, with the accompaniment of a loud ping from the bell on its shop door, entered The Red Triangle Stores, anxious to meet its owner. And why the anxiety? Because John Farley surely deserves an entry in the Guinness Book of Records. He told me that the shop had been here since 1934 and added quickly that 'I have not been here myself since 1934'. At first he was coy in letting on when he himself had joined the firm. I coaxed this out of him: 'I came in November 1952 and was only going to stay for six weeks. And I have been here ever since.'

John went on to tell me more about the business, with its slogan, 'THE SHOP OF A THOUSAND THINGS', describing its three parts: hardware, the model shop and the travel goods department, 'really three separate shops under the same roof'. And the red triangle? 'When it opened those many years ago the owner was trying to sell accumulators. At the end of his first week he had failed to make a single transaction. So he placed a neon red triangle on the top of the premises to attract customers. And that's how it got its name.'

I asked John whether he had a special affection after all these years for the Market. His reply was succinct: 'Not really. It is cold and miserable.' But he then went on to temper this somewhat stark statement: 'It is an interesting place with a variety of trades which is as it should be: four butchers, four greengrocers, four florists and, besides much else, one shop such as this. But in some respects it is archaic; it needs a man of vision to run it and to promote it. It cries out for a new look and I am sure that the stallholders would contribute to whatever the costs involved.' He reminded me that the States own it, and added, 'That is why this doesn't happen. They take the rent and do little for us.' And John added an interesting if irrelevant fact: 'Did you know that the floor of the Market slopes some five feet from south to north, and the reason for that? Before the site was roofed it was in use as a cattle market, and the slope allowed the urine to flow off into the gutters.'

I posed an inevitable question: was John Farley, after fifty-six years in the shop, contemplating retirement? His answer was brisk: 'When I get fed up. And I'm not fed up yet.' Indeed he is a man of many other interests which include presidency of the amateur dramatics Green Room Club and the fund-raising chairmanship of the Lions. He went on to tell me that he had been a States Member for six years from 1981, elected to represent the St Helier No.3 district and that it had been an honour to be a Deputy at that time. 'We weren't paid and I worked with some brilliant men in those days, including Ralph Vibert, John Le Marquand, Reg Jeune and Bernard Billington. You were humbled when in their presence. I doubt whether that would have been my feelings for the current batch of politicians. And then I was faced with a big decision: my business was suffering from the demands of my States work and I had to make the decision either to sell the shop or not stand for re-election. And I chose the latter'.

There is no doubting that John, after so many years at The Red Triangle Stores, is an optimist. 'We are unique in that we are an old-fashioned shop. We talk to the customers; we don't charge GST; we give out our shopping bags without charge; and we do an all-Island delivery service which is free. And we manage to survive.' I left this great survivor, cheered by his robust and forward-looking spirit.

~ THE ROYAL SQUARE TO WINDSOR CRESCENT...

~

Virtually next door to The Red Triangle Stores is the stall of Charles Dubois (Quality Meats) Ltd, and busy working at the chopping board was Jason Le Saint who came over to chat with me. He told me that he had gone straight in to butchery from school six years previously and that he had worked in wholesale before his present job. I cheekily asked him whether he still had all his fingers and he replied, 'I've been cut a couple of times. A lot of butchers will say that you are not a proper butcher until you cut yourself. It's inevitable; it's going to happen.' Did Jason have an affection for the Market. 'Oh yes,' he replied, 'I've worked in and around here for six years. I used to deliver the meat here to this stall before I joined Charles Dubois. You get your locals who are in every week, and the trade remains steady. Our busiest days are Fridays and Saturdays. And today is Monday, a prep. day when we get a lot done, making sure that we're prepared and ready to keep going through the week.'

I asked Jason to what extent they butchered the meat here, and he filled me in: 'The lamb we get as carcasses; the beef we get in as rump and loins. The country farm shops are doing Jersey beef these days and they get in the carcasses. But I have to tell you, I've never tried Jersey beef myself.'

Finally I asked Jason whether he was happy in his work. Again his answer was very positive: 'Yes. Some days do drag a bit when you are not too busy, but there are a lot of friendly people coming in and out of the Market all the time. And we get chatting.'

~

Having had my chat with Jason Le Saint, I moved across to another stall, the greengrocers Just William, and got into conversation with owner Billy Davies. Billy was another Hautlieu-educated boy, who had been intended for university to study Engineering. He told me that his parents, with a new grants system, could sadly not afford the fees. He had been working in the Market on Saturdays and in the holidays from the age of fourteen and on leaving school was offered a job with greengrocer Cyril Goaziou. 'I worked for Cyril for seven years,' Billy continued. 'He was a master of his trade. It was a great family business and he had come through the Occupation and some difficult times. I learned loads from him. Then at the age of twenty-five I thought of Engineering again but at the same time a Market business came up for sale and I took it on. I'm fifty now and Just William has been going for twenty-five years.'

Billy has a farm at St Martin and for years grew much of the produce that he sells in the Market. He told me more: 'I spent twenty-five years beating the drum of old-fashioned farming as close to organic as possible. It used up much time and emotion and we had to move on. Now as much of our produce as possible is grown locally for me; look at our exotic salads, all the beans and the varieties of spuds. We sell Jersey produce first and foremost; but it has to be the best. There was a time when the best produce grown in the Island was exported to the UK supermarkets, leaving us with the rubbish. All that has now fortunately changed; in the last few years the growers who are left have been and are absolutely superb.'

I next asked Billy whether the Market, in his view, was flourishing, whether it had a future. His response was optimistic and enthusiastic: 'The Market has the best position in Town and deserves to be made the centre of Town again. At present we have butchers, florists and greengrocers, all run by young people with families. I'm the oldest at fifty! While we here possess product knowledge, the out-of-town farm shops do everything and are masters of none of them. This younger Market base is coming through again and that is very healthy. Yes, we suffered cuts in numbers when Safeway opened and when parking scratch cards were introduced. But things are changing for the better: with environmental, 'green 'and 'buy local' issues we are getting more of our share, whereas the supermarkets sell nothing that is local. The numbers are coming back. But don't get me wrong: you have to work hard at it; it's not given to you; and you have to know your products.'

Did Billy, with his long involvement in the Central Market, have an affection for it? 'It is a Victorian building that could never be replaced and it should be kept in perfect condition. But none of the money which we pay in rents to the States has ever been properly invested in its upkeep. The politicians and civil servants don't admit to not spending money on the Market but continue to put off doing work on it. Think of all that money they have recently spent on Mont Orgueil. Only a fraction of the numbers visit it that go through here, with three to four thousand coming on a Saturday into what is surely the most beautiful building in the Island.'

And a final thought from greengrocer Billy Davies? 'Most markets in England have gone, similarly in France. As long as we have young people taking up stalls, then that's brilliant. If you work hard in the Market you'll flourish and earn a good living for your family.'

~

I had one more Central Market port of call before moving on, and that was to the office of Richard MacKenzie, St Helier's Town Centre Manager. Richard, educated at Gresham's School in Norfolk, was born and brought up in London. After school he went straight into retail, joining BHS where his grandfather had been Managing Director. Ever wanting to manage a BHS store by the seaside, his ambition was realised when he came to take over the St Helier branch in 1995. 'They had all the flags out for me – bunting everywhere. I thought this a real Jersey welcome until I was told that it was the fiftieth anniversary of the Liberation.'

Richard was manager of BHS here for ten years. 'I retired in 2005 and we went to live in the New Forest, but after two and a half years my wife said that she would like to go back to Jersey. I said, "Of course, darling" and back we came.'

Richard was then appointed Town Centre Manager and I wanted to know to whom he answered. 'Look at my business card,' he replied. 'It carries two crests at the top: that of the States and of the Parish. And the Chamber of Commerce is about to be added.' And what was his job specification? 'I used to pooh-pooh mission statements but have drafted this.' Richard reached for a piece of paper and read this out to me: 'To create a first-class environment in the town centre of St Helier that is clean, safe, easy to access and enjoyable to visit, maximising the prosperity of all businesses and enhancing the quality of life of all those both living in the centre and visiting it.' He added this: 'Everything I do relates back to that; it involves much communication, talking to a lot of people and attempting to pull all the strings together.'

With enthusiasm, Richard continued: 'These are the sort of questions I ask: How clean is the Town? Was it a safe and happy experience to be in it? Were you able to park easily? I am also involved currently with the idea of a St Helier Festival, with perhaps school involvement, and trying to promote the story of our patron saint. I want St Helier to be a vibrant, exciting place and possibly harnessing the youth with their music. The talent on the Island is exceptional and could be tapped. And we are promoting alfresco in the summer. BHS incidentally was the first store to put out tables and chairs, first from April to October, but it's now all the year round.'

I wondered what Richard MacKenzie's views were on the proposals for a big financial centre with retail outlets to be built on the Waterfront. Would it mean empty offices elsewhere and empty shops in the centre? I sensed that Richard has his eye on the nearer future: 'My concern is to make Town a vibrant and exciting place. As a retailer I would need a huge incentive to trade on the Waterfront rather than in King Street. I think King Street will remain a very strong retail area and elsewhere a secondary retail location. The Waterfront plans are a fair way off realisation and my goals are somewhat closer.'

And more pedestrianisation in Town? 'Pedestrianisation is always advantageous for shoppers but it can be a problem for the person coming in to Town. It has to be combined with other devices such as perhaps a hopper bus service to take traffic out of the centre. Parking too is an emotive issue. What about an Oyster Card making it cheaper for people from the west to use a western car park and those from the east an eastern car park, cutting out cross-Town travel?'

Richard MacKenzie's final remark to me was that so much of his job consisted of going out and talking to people. With that we left his office in the Central Market together and strolled up to King Street where a television crew was waiting to interview him for its local evening news bulletin.

~

I now made for Beresford Street with, on the right, the Victoria Club where I had lunched some time before with Tristan Lewis. Brett is not kind about the club's appearance, describing this 1894 building as 'a curious imposing symmetrical high Victorian block' and considering its porch 'very heavy and unclassical'. I was heading across the road for the Beresford Market – the Fish Market, built in 1854 and restored in 1873 and 1936 – with its pleasant and dignified granite archway. What is it about fish markets that is so enticing and attractive? Jersey's is surely one of the best, with its four big stalls and their alluring and comprehensive piscine displays. I am a reasonably regular customer of Fin & Feather Ltd (Fish, Game and Poultry Suppliers), noticed some sea trout on the slab, watched while a specimen was expertly filleted for me and looked forward to the evening's supper.

Just across from Fin and Feather is Relish Food & Wine. I also sometimes patronise them for their Drappier champagne and their fine cheese selection, and I popped in to have a chat during a lull in trading with the manager and company secretary, John Hunter. John is relatively new to Jersey and new to the business of selling speciality food. He came to the Island in 2004 and had been for twenty-nine years an officer in the RAF's administration branch, coming out as a Wing Commander. He is an enthusiast for the Market: 'It's fantastic and, if people want quality, then that is what we have here. As to thoughts of the Market moving down to the Waterfront, that would be an absolute mistake. It would kill the centre of Town. Yes, there has recently been a slight dropping off of customers; the credit crunch hasn't helped. But let's leave the Market where it is and let it grow.'

John has another string to his bow: he is a member of the Honorary Police, a Constable's Officer in St John. I asked him why he had volunteered and he told me this: 'When we first arrived we lived at Sion, and my idea was to retire totally and play golf. But I got fed up; I am not a house husband. I noticed from the *JEP* that they were short of volunteers; I contacted the St John Parish Hall; and the Constable came down to see me. We had been made very welcome on coming to the Island, and here was the opportunity to give something back to the community.'

And the commitment? 'It's not huge. We have a week on duty every six weeks and are of course called in at other times. I enjoy it immensely. My colleagues are such a nice bunch of chaps. It's a superb system, and this was shown when there was a big hillside fire at Bouley Bay. The duty centenier called me – I was actually at the Battle of Flowers dinner – and said that there was a problem in Trinity. Could I come and help? Well, the Honorary Police from all over the Island turned out and, when we had a break, there were the Constable and his wife at the Parish Hall making tea and coffee for the evacuees.'

My last question for John Hunter was to ask him how he had taken to living in

Fish Market

Jersey. His reply could not have been more positive: 'It was the first time that I had been to the Island when we came in 2004. It's a lovely place with lovely people. Some say that you get claustrophobic and need at times to get off. Not so with me; I love it here.'

~

I came out of the Fish Market by its Minden Place entrance and turned right, making my way to Phillips Street and a favourite venue of mine, Jersey Arts Centre, opened in 1982 (its theatre was completed four years later), with its external architecture described by Boots as 'elegant, if minimal'. I wanted to have a chat with the Arts Centre's Director, Daniel Austin, knocked on his door, interrupted his deskwork and over the next hour gained a very useful perception of him and his responsibilities. Daniel came to the Island and took up his post in 2001, having initially trained as an actor. He spent the whole of the '90s in three concurrent jobs as actor, teacher and director and from 1999 to 2001 was Artistic Director of The Castle Theatre and Arts Centre in Wellingborough.

I began our chat by putting forward the notion that Daniel was more keen on and thus promoted drama while his predecessor as Arts Centre Director, Rod McLoughlin, had weighted the programmes in his day with a greater emphasis on music. Daniel gave me this response: 'That is a myth which has grown up during my tenure. Look back on the balance of the programme during Rod's thirteen years at the helm and you will find it was as balanced as it is now. Rod was as interested in theatre, drama and dance as I am in music.'

I told Daniel that at some of the chamber music events attendance was somewhat below the 250 capacity of the theatre. Was Jersey particularly philistine, when a world-famous pianist or string quartet managed to attract an audience of only 100? Daniel's reply was a helpful insight into his philosophy as Director: 'You have to remember that Jersey has a fixed population – 90,000 – plus visitors; so much is on offer for them, be it the Arts Centre, the Opera House, sports clubs and so on. If there are forty people wanting to see a particular genre of event, then we should programme it. Of course it matters in terms of box office receipts that the audience is large, but we must find the balance, with popular events balancing the less popular. Our doors should always be open for people to come and experience an aspect of the arts for the first time. Our focus has to be on providing a really broad programme of music, drama, comedy and dance. And concerning numbers, our average house for drama is between 80 and 120. Over the last few years we have in fact sustained our audiences.'

Daniel and I then discussed his States subsidy – a revenue grant from the Department of Education, Sport and Culture – which is supplemented by box office receipts and income from other Arts Centre activities as well as sponsorship.

'Yes, we could always do with more funding, but we have been good over more than twenty-five years at balancing the books and putting together inventive programmes.'

I wondered what Daniel's views were on relations with the Opera House. Should there perhaps be the one director for both? He replied in this way: 'It is important that what is on offer at the Arts Centre, the Opera House and Fort Regent is complementary; we are not in competition. The question of common direction has been around for a long time, but what is good about the present set-up is this: currently you have more than one person's vision and at the moment you have different venues with unique identities, and this results in greater variety.'

I am always interested to find out what those relatively new to Jersey think of the Island and broached my oft-asked question: what did Daniel consider was the essence of this island community? He replied, remarking on Jersey's natural beauty and its relative peace and safety and then went on, if not to qualify this, to dig a little deeper into the matter: 'It can be frightening everywhere if you peel back the surface and discover that prejudice, racism and greed can exist. What is great about Jersey is its multi-cultural aspect. It depends whom one is talking to, but there is tolerance and intolerance, awareness and lack of awareness wherever you go. Besides our great sense of community and friendliness there is also, perhaps influenced by the finance industry, much wealth and with it some greed and prejudice. And maybe that is where the arts can play their part and provide the means to bridge the divisions and narrow the extremes. When we celebrated our first twenty years in 2002, Sir Philip Bailhache, whose contribution to its founding was immense, said that the thing about the Arts Centre was that, whether you were wearing jeans and a T-shirt or a jacket and tie, you were always welcome. That spirit I would never want to change.'

~

Leaving the Arts Centre I returned to Bath Street where I bumped in to Advocate Christopher Lakeman whom I know slightly. It was lunchtime and we decided to make for the Bistro Central where, over food for us both with a glass of wine for me and a Coke for Chris, I got out the Dictaphone and pressed the recording button. First I discovered something of Christopher's roots: the divorce of his parents when he was five, Janvrin Primary School and then Le Rocquier followed at fourteen by Hautlieu – in his words 'a breath of fresh air' – ending up as Head Boy. He read English and French Law at the University of Kent at Canterbury, where he was chairman of the University Conservative Association, before reading for the bar at the Middle Temple, briefly practising in London and then returning to Jersey in 1992 to the law firm of Pickersgill and Le Cornu. Chris, now mostly involved in commercial and trust litigation, told me that in those days one tended to be a general practitioner 'before everybody began specialising'.

Christopher Lakeman was a States Member from 1999 until he retired from political life in 2006 and I wanted to learn more about this. He had much to tell me: 'I came second in the senatorial elections to Stuart Syvret and enjoyed some aspects of my political career. But there were some dirty tricks played on me concerning my personal life, and this was tough. I found myself in something of a surreal world. Let me give you an example. There was the business of the unaccountability of States loans to agriculture. When I took up this issue I was absolutely hounded for daring to challenge a senior States Member on the matter. Then a person in receipt of one of these loans tragically committed suicide. Four hours after the death, someone rang me up and blamed me for it. In the States I found a lot of petty jealousies and this complacent attitude that things should always be done "the Jersey way". And then I was finding that one was for ever on duty – getting paranoid if I went out on a Sunday morning to buy a paper without having shaved. One attracted a degree of public interest, constantly having to be on one's guard. In the end I resigned from the States, not wanting, through pressure of too much political work, to be known as a failed lawyer.'

Chris told me that he had given evidence twice to the Clothier Commission on Jersey's machinery of government which had reported in December 2000. What were his thoughts on its recommendations and what had happened since? 'I was generally in favour of it, believing that it would end this business of States committees communicating by love-ins. I was one of the Young Turks rooting for reform. Two factors contributed to Clothier being far from implemented. There was the intervention of the Bailiff which I considered damaging and improper and there was the Clothier Commission itself which set out the way forward but to some extent failed to back up what it proposed. We now have ministerial government but no electoral reform. It seems impossible to get any sort of consensus among States Members for the latter; it is like wading through treacle. So two big regrets: the failure to deal with electoral reform and the ways in which, when accepted, the principles of ministerial government were diluted.'

Did the answer lie in Jersey espousing political parties? 'You cannot invent political parties like that,' Chris replied, 'and in the past Jersey political parties almost wrecked the judiciary by politicising the role of the Jurats. I have no real answer to the absence of parties; it does mean that there is no way of developing policy other than on the hoof. And a problem with the States is that the longer the legislation, the shorter the debate; the more complex the issue, the less discussion.'

Now Chris is something of an authority on the matter of Jersey's relations with the United Kingdom, and I could not let him get up from the table before I raised this issue. Was Sir Philip Bailhache right, I asked, in considering it quite likely that Jersey would be completely independent in fifty years' time? Chris's answer was interesting: 'It is true that HM-in-Council acts as the ultimate guarantor of good government of Jersey, but the British parliament has foresworn any power over us. As to independence there might one day be a case for it, but I believe that the question of independence is secondary to the matter of us getting our own house in order. Maybe independence in fifty years' time; but there are internal structures – for example involving the parishes more and division of legislative power and scrutiny versus the power of ministers – which require our attention. And lack of co-operation with Guernsey makes independence less a possibility. Despite such a community of interests between the two bailiwicks, there is far too often no meeting of minds.'

I had one final issue to bring up – the Opera House, where Christopher Lakeman was until April 2009 Chairman of its board. Chris was frank: 'Personally it was the most challenging matter that I had ever been involved in. When I took over as Chairman we had an accumulated deficit of £294,000. That was in 2004 and we turned that round to the tune of £400,000 with another healthy surplus for 2008. But there was much backbiting, and I was on the receiving end of offensive correspondence. But we rescued the Opera House, with its happy staff, wonderful volunteers and a varied programme.'

It had been a fulfilling lunch in more ways than one; the tape had nearly run out and we had almost outstayed the Bistro Central's welcome. I said my farewells to one of Jersey's most interesting lawyers and we went our separate ways.

~

At the top of Bath Street and on its west side is what was once the Odeon cinema, built in 1952. It was the first Odeon constructed after the second world war and Brett puts it neatly: 'A very odd piece of Great West Road architecture; the use of boiled eggs/pingpong balls in sixes as ornaments is particularly intriguing'. I called in, almost gate-crashed, on a significant occasion: the very night that Deputy Kevin Lewis was giving up his lease on what for the previous four years had been the New Forum, and with the last films ever being shown on its screens. Radio and television were there to interview Kevin and I waited my turn; Tina, long-serving box-office lady, came up at the end of her shift to kiss him and wish him goodbye. It was all rather emotional, and I felt something of an interloper. But I was quickly put at my ease and, with the media having completed their business and departed, Kevin Lewis was generous to me with his time and conversation.

I first learned of his early life and career: Bristol-born in 1953 and coming to Jersey in 1978 to run the Forum Cinema. He was chief projectionist there until it closed. He then went to work at the Odeon where one day he received a phone call from the BBC who were taking over the Forum for the filming of *Bergerac*: would Kevin help them out? That was the start of his ten-year stretch as locations manager for the famous series. At the same time his cinema work continued. He explained: 'I bought the Ciné de France company in 1985 and took over the lease of the cinema based at the Hotel de France complex. This was the heyday of Jersey tourism and many visitors thought that the Ciné de France was a French movie art house! As we expanded from one screen to four we changed the name to Cinécentre.'

Detail of former Odeon Cinema

I asked Kevin whether he had a special affection for the Odeon. 'Yes, I have an affection for all cinemas,' he replied. 'There's nothing worse than to see an old cinema boarded up, and it gave me a great kick to bring this one back to life four years ago. What happened was this: when Cineworld opened on the Waterfront, Jersey with its population of 90,000 ended up with eighteen screens – four at Cinécentre, four at the Odeon and ten at Cineworld. There must have been more screens per head than anywhere else in the world. It spelt the end of Cinécentre and then the Odeon. One night I was walking the dog down Bath Street, saw the boarded-up building and decided to give it a go. Le Masurier were now the owners and leased it to me at a favourable rent and, after a struggle, Odeon agreed to lift the restrictive covenant on the cinema and gave me the green light to open. We have run it on a break-even basis as a community cinema and tonight the lease comes to an end.'

Kevin Lewis stood for and entered the States in 2005 and became Assistant Minister in the Transport and Technical Services Department in 2008. What, I wondered, were his political priorities? 'I fight hard for the rights of pensioners and for long-term health benefits. And if I could wave a wand, I would want to promote a town park which is at least in the pipeline. As to Transport, it has been a very steep learning curve: Jersey traffic is terrible; we have got to change people's love of the car and get more of them back onto the buses. And incidentally, some of the fact-finding for my new responsibilities has, to say the least, been interesting: I have been up to the top of the Bellozane chimney and it's windy up there and it sways a bit. There were a few moments at 300 feet when my knuckles were a little bit white and there was just a fragile bit of scaffolding between me and the drop to the ground.'

By this time Kevin and I had been joined by his wife Isabella, here at the cinema with her husband for its obsequies. Isabella had an interesting and touching story to tell: 'I was a Swedish journalist and television presenter and came to Jersey in order to interview John Nettles and Terence Alexander (who played Charlie Hungerford in the *Bergerac* series). I saw this man, the locations manager – lovely and friendly – and fell for him in a big way. And for our wedding in St Helier the Beeb let us borrow Bergerac's 1956 Triumph Roadster. The car was parked outside and a crowd gathered to see the married couple emerge. They got a shock: everybody thought that John Nettles was getting married, but it was the two of us.'

Towards the end of our conversation Kevin Lewis said to me: 'I have two passions – politics and film.' And the future; what were his film plans? 'Well,' he answered, 'I've been running the Jersey Film Festival for seventeen years; we've had a summer open air event at Durrell and *Shakespeare in the Square* in the Royal Square, and we've settled into Howard Davis Park with the screen hoisted on the bandstand. I would love to expand all this.' And a St Helier art-house cinema in the future? 'It's certainly a possibility despite our not being in the UK and thus not eligible for any grants.'

Isabella had the last word on this rather sad, final evening: 'We haven't heard the last of Kevin and cinema in Jersey.' I am fairly sure that she was right.

~

My route now took me north up David Place and then right into Gas Place and on to Oxford Road. Here one is in that part of St Helier, with its terraces of Victorian houses opening on to the pavements, that makes it a special town, one that does not empty in the evenings when the financiers get in their company cars and drive out to the rural parishes. So many people live within half a mile or so of the Market and this is one of the reasons why it continues to be such an important and lively retail centre.

Oxford Road brings one up alongside Stopford Road's Masonic Temple. Now Brett is not kind about this building that dates from 1864. He describes it in these words: 'Extraordinarily heavy and forbidding Corinthian stucco monster'. The Freemasons' own leaflet is more complimentary: '[It] is one of the most attractive buildings of its type throughout the United Kingdom. It is constructed of brick and cement with granite facings in pure Corinthian style, classical in appearance and beautiful as regards detail'. I now sought out someone who, better qualified than anyone else, could tell me about Freemasonry in Jersey and Freemasonry in general. Dennis Perrin became a Mason in 1949 and has held high Masonic office, being presented in 2000 with the Grand Master's (HRH the Duke of Kent's) Order of Service to Masonry, an honour held at any one time by only twelve recipients. But before we talked about Freemasonry I wanted to know something of Dennis's long life. He is a Jerseyman, born in 1920, who after his school education worked in the Jersey Post Office. War service took him to many countries of the Middle East, and after that he worked in the Post Office in London before entering the Colonial Office and then the Foreign Office with postings in Vienna, Frankfurt, Paris, Geneva and elsewhere before his retirement and return to Jersey in 1973.

I asked Dennis about the Masonic Temple, and he told me more: 'It's regarded as an outstanding Masonic structure with a beautiful interior. But we have the usual trouble with buildings of this age; it is costing a fortune to maintain – to keep out the wind and water – and, as with similar organisations, our active membership and hence our finances are not as strong as they used to be. In pursuit of their vendetta against the Freemasons, early in the Occupation the Nazis sent special troops to sack the building and to ship the main furnishings and possessions to Berlin where they were used to set up an anti-Masonic exhibition. I have been privileged to play my part in restoring our library and museum after this terrible desecration.'

Dennis then detailed something of Freemasonry in Jersey: 'There are eleven lodges and they all use the Temple for their meetings. Nearly every night there is something happening, and we have our own dining facilities with living-in caterer and caretaker. At a Masonic meeting there is first the ceremony, the ritual based on the ancient stonemasons' craft when in ancient times a level of proficiency had to be reached before admission to the lodge; then we discuss the business matters of the lodge before dining together.'

This was my next question: how many Masons were there in Jersey? Dennis replied: 'There was a great boom in the 1920s and '30s. In those days in a population of, say, 50,000 there would have been a membership of well over 1000. Now, with different and demanding professional lifestyles, there are just under 600, with perhaps 350 of them being active.' And the purpose of Freemasonry? 'I put it this way,' responded Dennis, 'Freemasonry is not a religion. It is open to men of any race or religion who subscribe to a belief in a Supreme Being. We try to follow three main principles: showing respect and tolerance for the opinions of others; behaving with kindness and understanding to everyone and not just to fellow Masons; and practising charity not only for our own but for the community at large.'

I suspect that Dennis Perrin was expecting my next question: why the secrecy? And the fact that he was chatting to me so freely was an indication as to how this has changed in recent years. He continued, 'Our Grand Master, the Duke of Kent, has done much to encourage greater openness. For instance we are much more ready nowadays to publicise our donations to non-Masonic charitable bodies, all such donations incidentally having been contributed entirely by members of the organisation. And we now regularly hold open days for members of the public and are anxious to be recognised as playing a full role in the life of the local community. We even these days have an officially approved tie bearing the easily recognised Masonic insignia of the square and compasses which can be worn by members at any time and not just at meetings. As to the Masonic handshake, there are books on sale that will tell you all about it. The truth is that in the past we have been our own worst enemies, and it has now all changed.' But what about Masonry and supposed favouritism towards its own members? Dennis was firm in his response: 'If a Freemason used his membership to promote his own or anyone's else's business, professional or personal, he would be utterly condemned. It is absolutely contrary to the conditions on which any individual seeks admission to Freemasonry. Also steps would be taken to discipline an individual trying to use his Masonic membership in attempting to advance his own interest.'

I was very grateful to Dennis Perrin, almost a nonagenarian and a considerable and respected authority on all matters Masonic, for his frank and full information. His wife's coffee had been excellent too. I gave him my warm thanks and made my way further up Oxford Road.

~

I had never previously set foot in Springfield, its grounds and stadium. For many years in the past the site was used for exhibitions and shows; the Beatles and the Rolling Stones played in its old hall; and it was also the headquarters of the Royal Jersey Agricultural & Horticultural Society. Indeed the one definite thing that I did know about the old Springfield was the fact that in the 1950s my father-in-law, Frank Perrée, had sadly lost his hand there in an accident while demonstrating a piece of agricultural machinery.

Springfield Stadium Sports Centre in its present incarnation dates from 1997 and I called on Stephen Dunford, its Assistant Manager, to find out more. We sat in the Stadium café and over a coffee he told me that he was a Jerseyman who had gained a university degree in Leisure Management before taking up his current post eight years ago. He filled me in: 'It's a very varied job, dealing a lot with the public of course. We have a full-time staff of four and four part-timers. We're a very popular part of the States provision for leisure, open from 6.30 a.m. to 10 at night, with the weekends 9 to 5.'

Stephen then gave me a tour of the facilities: people sweating away in the gym; the sports hall upstairs with opportunities for football, badminton, netball and so on; and then the Blue Room where courses in pilates, yoga, salsa aerobics and more are on offer through the week. Outside there is the spectator stand and the pitch for the Jersey football teams. I am sure that Stephen was right when he told me this: 'The facilities we have in Jersey for sports and fitness are unparalleled anywhere in the UK.' And when I admitted to Stephen that I occasionally went and had a swim at Quennevais, he suggested that I should have an Active Card which I could use at Quennevais, Springfield and Fort Regent for all the classes, the gyms and the swimming pool. Feeling suddenly just a tad tired, I gave him my thanks and limped away.

~

From Springfield Stadium I walked towards David Place along St Mark's Road. Here, with its mixture of two- and three-storey houses in Georgian, Regency and Victorian styles, one is once again in that more northerly part of St Helier which was developed in the early 19th century in response to its influx of prosperous residents from the United Kingdom. Nowadays the area is characterised by so many properties in multi-occupancy and a plethora of residents' parked cars. At the junction with David Place stands St Mark's church. I know it well, having been its organist for a couple of years and, as a campanologist, being well acquainted with its peal of six bells. St Mark's was built in 1845 when burgeoning congregations were too great for the parish church alone. It has to be said that from the outside it is a dreary building with its all-over sand cement rendering; but its external saving grace is its tower and spire. The interior is more inspiring: a tall nave and galleries with a roof carried on rows of wooden columns. And it has a fine two-manual organ (with an impressive and extremely loud trumpet rank *en chamade* - the pipes horizontal and outside the organ case) which, with a then strong choir to accompany, I much enjoyed playing for services.

Next door to St Mark's church is The Deanery and just round the corner into Val Plaisant is an architectural delight, Windsor Crescent. It is a charming scheme

St Mark's Church

of eight houses built in 1835 and all painted in the same basic pattern of black and white. Regency details abound in the overhanging eves, the curved metal canopies over the ground floor windows and the slender fluted columns which support them. Both Brett and Boots are full of praise and the former has this description: 'A very fine symmetrical terrace, arranged in a half moon around a nice private garden.' By chance I know the owner of No.1, Clive Barton, and sought him out at his Moore Stephens office in Peter Street.

Windsor Crescent

We first talked about Windsor Crescent, his home for twenty-six years. 'To me', said Clive, 'it's fantastic. I have always been something of a towny; it takes me a minute to get to work on my scooter and in the summer I get home and have a swim in our pool at the back. But the sadness for me is this: ours is the only complete house in the Crescent; the rest are doctors' and dentists' surgeries and flats. We're the only one with the original lead-lined wooden gutters. Sadly some of the other houses have been vandalised internally; ours fortunately has the original mahogany spiral staircase with the mother of pearl lozenge in the rail at the bottom. For me it is a wonderful oasis of peace and yet still in the middle of town with that nice sense of life passing by outside.'

I did not want to miss this opportunity of talking more with Clive Barton, a man who lives the fullest life, about other things. He was born in Sutton in Surrey and came as a boarder to Victoria College, being admitted by the headmaster, so he said, because they were looking for a good goalkeeper. Later offered a trial with Chelsea when Tommy Docherty was manager, he opted instead for accountancy and joined Moore Stephens in the City of London, attracted by the prospects offered by its branch in Bermuda. 'So I joined them,' he told me, 'but it took me another twelve years before I made it out there.'

Clive came back to Jersey in 1974, having just qualified, and joined the Moore Stephens office of four people. He became its Senior Partner in 1978. He is now in charge of Moore Stephens's Jersey, Guernsey, Gibraltar and Isle of Man operations, with a total staff of some 200. In addition he is a Director and past Chairman of Moore Stephens Europe Limited. With the global crisis and credit crunch all around us, I got Clive to tell me a little about his job. 'What we are involved in, as are firms like us, is the preservation of wealth. These are extraordinary times and safe havens are not quite as safe as they were. Most of the people we deal with are sophisticated investors with wide interests; we have clients involved with property, film finance, Greek shipping and so on; a diverse client base. Like the poor, the rich are always with us. I must tell you this: there is a rather butch Texan woman who comes over once a year with her City investment adviser. He does everything by formulae and computer programmes; he's been quite good up till now but has fallen down a bit this year as you would expect. He had the temerity to tell our American lady that she had only lost £330m. She flew off the handle: "£330 f****** million?" Then he made it worse by saying to her, "Well, you still have £900m," to which she replied, "I know, but it is f****** terrible." As to Jersey's general position in all this, I see some tightening of the belt, but I don't see the core offering of Jersey as being any less attractive. We still offer a product which is admired globally and our finance industry is in relatively good health.'

Clive Barton's other interests are legion. I first encountered him when I was a Governor of Victoria College and he came on the Board as Chairman. He is also a past Chairman of the Highlands College Board of Governors, remains a member of it and speaks in very generous terms about our island's further education establishment: 'It is such a diverse institution – almost brick-laying to brain surgery. And of course one can study for a degree there these days. Also I think of the young people between sixteen and eighteen; lots of them can't wait to leave school, and Highlands sweeps them up into its embrace, giving them much guidance and injecting value into their lives. As you can sense, I am a big fan of the place.'

Clive has also been Treasurer of the Société Jersiaise for over a decade and continues to give very valuable service to the parish of St Helier as one of its Procureurs du Bien Public. He told me more about this: 'Originally I was rung up and told that, if I let my name go forward, it would mean an afternoon or so every month. Well, it has turned out to be a much greater commitment. I am supposed to be the keeper of the Constable's conscience and am elected by the parish to see that the books are straight and the Constable is under control. Yes, I enjoy the commitment, and all these things that I do I would never undertake half-heartedly.'

Clive Barton's industry and involvement in so much left me, many years into my retirement, almost exhausted in contemplating the scale and scope of his considerable activities, both professional and voluntary. What was the secret of this busy resident of No.1 Windsor Crescent? He gave me the answer: 'My two mottoes for life are "You know the rules" and "If it isn't fun, it probably isn't worth doing".'

5

The Royal Square to Victoria College by way of Morier House, Green Street and St Saviour's Road

For this my fifth stroll round St Helier I headed for the eastern end of the Royal Square, crossed Halkett Place and entered the impressive portals of Morier House where several States departments including the States Greffe and the Law Officers have their base. A plaque on the left of the entrance says this:

> This stone was laid by
> Sir Philip Bailhache
> Bailiff of Jersey
> 14th July 1997
> States of Jersey

Inside the building is another:

> To commemorate the opening
> of Morier House by
> Her Royal Highness the Princess Royal
> 23rd July 1998

Suitably impressed, I was given a visitor's badge and took the lift, worthy in its gleam and glass of the elevator of a five-star hotel, to the second floor in order to meet with Michael de la Haye, the Greffier of the States. Michael first told me something of Morier House itself, built just over a decade ago on the site of a hotel that then became a bank. He then spoke of his early life and career: 'Yes, I am a Jerseyman, educated at Victoria College. I went on to Nottingham University and read French and Linguistics. After that there were two years in Tunisia teaching English as a foreign language and four years in the university in Clermont-Ferrand as a *lecteur*. By this time I was married with two young sons, and we decided to come back to Jersey. I first worked as an immigration officer and then moved to

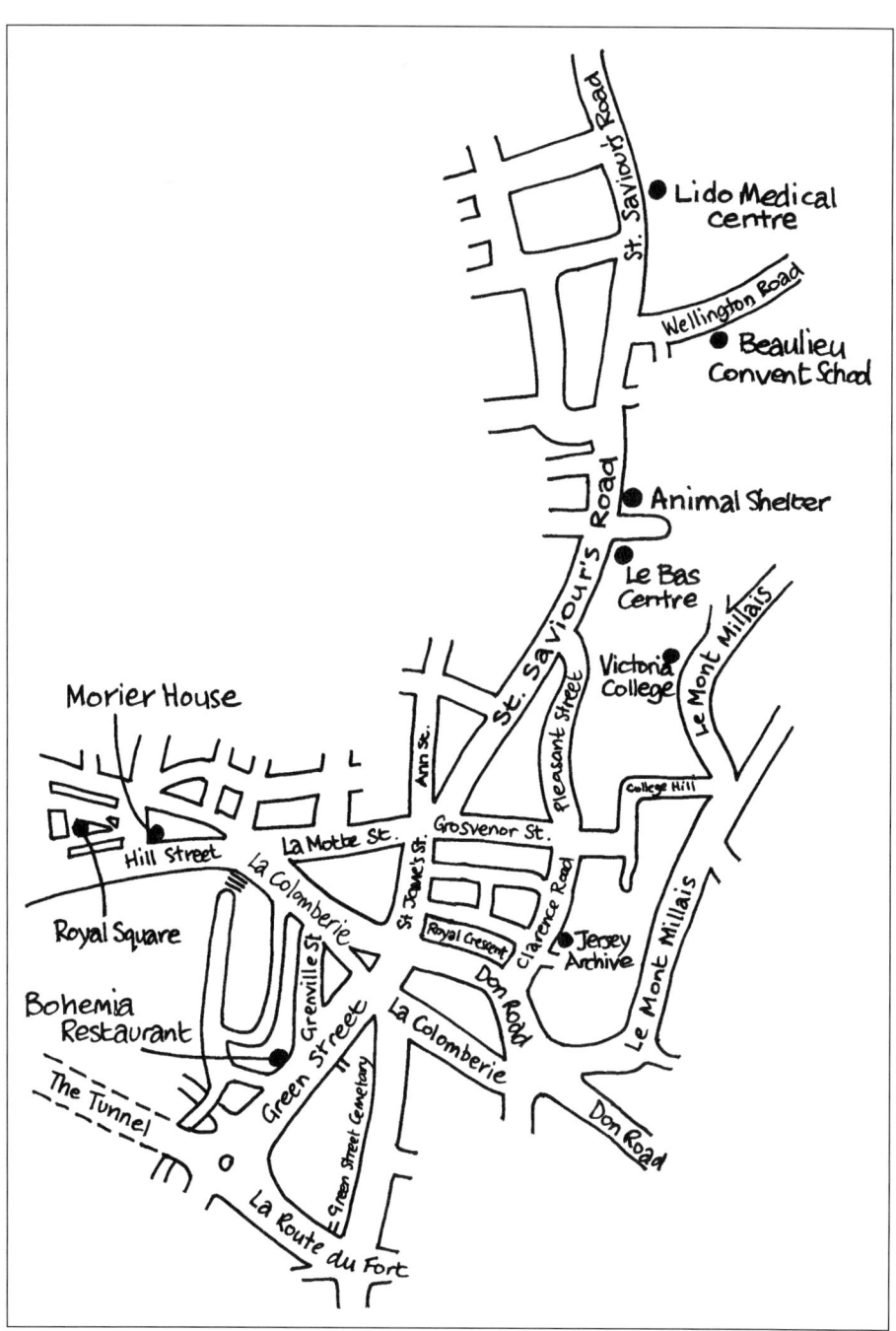

the Attorney-General's department as its Chief Clerk. I became Assistant Greffier in 1999, Deputy Greffier in 2000 and was appointed Greffier of the States in 2002.'

I was anxious to know exactly what Michael de la Haye's job was. He obliged: 'In other jurisdictions I might be termed the Clerk of the Parliament. The overarching thing is this: the States Greffe provides the administration for the States Assembly to enable it to meet. We provide the documentation and the order paper. The propositions and reports are prepared and printed here. We assist the Bailiff, working with him and giving advice when required. I would stress this: we work very closely with and serve all fifty-three States Members. They come in to see us or e-mail us and we give them help over questions and propositions. Also with our new system of ministerial government we provide the support for the scrutiny panels. And at times I preside over the States, and this is unusual for an official to do so. I am usually only in the chair for the odd hour or half-hour. Normally I or the Deputy Greffier sits in front of the Bailiff and he can consult us on points of procedure. Being in the chair is interesting: matters arise and there is sometimes the need for instant decision-making when a ruling is required.'

Michael quite correctly could not be drawn by me when I asked him about possible reform of the States. His response was sensibly diplomatic: 'It would be devastating for the role of the Greffier and his department if we were not seen as totally impartial. It is so important that Members can come and talk in confidence to us and know that that will be respected. In the morning I can be discussing with the Chief Minister some proposition or other and in the afternoon be with a backbench Member opposed to the Chief Minister and who may wish to bring an amendment to the same proposition. Neither of them will know of my conversation with the other; it is fundamental that we can give an equal level of advice and information to any States Member.'

The Greffier of the States did go on to tell me that his department had worked closely with the States Privileges and Procedures Committee on reform matters, doing much background research concerning other jurisdictions and looking into such issues as voter turn-out. 'The problem in the past with reform,' added Michael, 'seemed to be this: most Members may have had his or her view on the matter, with ten favouring this, ten that and ten the other, but it is has always been hard for all fifty-three in the States to reach a consensus. Bear this in mind: our legislature has an unusual and unique structure with three categories of member within one unicameral parliament. For example, some consider the all-Island position of Senator important, some see the position of the Connétables as a vital link with the parishes and some favour the Deputies being related to the parishes. This is a difficult starting point from which to take reform forward.'

Finally I voiced my presumptuous thoughts that the States of Jersey had the characteristics of both a town council and a national parliament. Michael de la

Haye's response was firm: 'It is not a local council; it is our law-making body. That Jersey has its own legislature is of the greatest importance and this concept must be championed and defended. The fact that we have our own parliament is fundamental to the Island's whole constitutional and historical position.'

~

On the same floor as the States Greffe are the offices of Jersey's Data Protection Commissioner, Emma Martins, and I called in to see her. It was perhaps predictable that I first brought up the fact that she has a famous father, John Nettles, none other than Bergerac himself and highly regarded by so many Jersey people. Emma fortunately did not mind my immediate reference to him and answered me in this way: 'I am hugely proud of my father and what he has achieved. During my childhood in North London there were times when he was out of work, 'resting' as actors term it. *Bergerac* rescued him and I remember clearly the day when my father got the job. We were having a meal in a restaurant in Aldwych and Dad went upstairs to take a phone call from his agent. He had been given the part and hence the prospect of one year's steady work. That all happened in 1981 and the following year he was out here filming and I at the age of eleven or twelve would join him in the school holidays. And the truth is that I fell in love with Jersey hook, line and sinker. I found the Island beautiful and free of the fumes and many of the social problems of the big city. At the age of seventeen I came over for good and, as they say, the rest is history.'

How, I enquired, had she come to her present important position? 'At the first opportunity I moved into the public sector; that was in Planning at South Hill. Then I worked for Jersey Police as an administration manager, and part of that post in those early days was to develop the Force's data protection policy. I came here as deputy to the Data Protection Registrar in 2000 and succeeded as Commissioner in 2006.'

Emma Martins now told me what her job embraced. 'Think of the data footprint that you leave in your life every day: CCTV in the streets, the swipe card to get into a particular building, your bank account, your mobile phone, your medical records at the doctor and the hospital. There needs to be control as to who has access to this information and to its security. You as a citizen have fundamental rights that require protection and the law is there as a framework for this. It is a deeply serious matter when and if data gets into the wrong hands.'

And what actually was her role? She replied: 'I engage with government concerning issues of privacy. We put a lot of effort into talking to the various departments where these issues are paramount: the social services and the Police for example. You see, some of the high-risk areas are medical and police records, welfare issues and the like. And every day – several hundred a year – we receive complaints of data misuse and are active in addressing them.'

I wondered whether there was any conflict between data protection on the one hand and freedom of information on the other. Emma answered me in this way: 'The two concepts work well together. Take this example: if Joe Bloggs, aged fourteen and living at 4 Acacia Avenue is drunk on a Friday night, that is a data protection matter. The policy that the Police put into place, however, concerning drunken behaviour is in the public domain. Of course when the issues are people in the public eye and their private conduct, then that gets complicated. But for most Jersey citizens there is a clear line: how much they get in welfare or any matter at their GP surgery, for them that is private; but the overall strategy of States departments and how they deal with, say, social or medical issues, is a matter of public interest.'

And data protection and the future? The Commissioner was far from complacent: 'Our single biggest social, cultural and legal challenge is the internet. There is no problem in Jersey's government determining the way that cars should be driven or how alcohol is sold. But suddenly with the internet there is a hive of activity lying outside our jurisdiction. For example our young people with Facebook and the like are putting themselves on the internet; and employers increasingly do Google searches on prospective employees. Twitter and Facebook: these are alien languages to me and we risk losing the ability to communicate traditionally. As a mother I am disturbed by those websites that can get my child to give personal details and photographs. And it very much concerns me as a regulator. The internet is a wonderful tool but I consider that socially and culturally we are yet to have a proper debate as to how it is developing. My opposite number in the UK recently said that we are possibly sleep-walking into a surveillance society where everything is open. Yes, this may be a job for government to tackle, but then how far can government go without being seen as a dictatorship?'

With these disturbing considerations in mind, I asked the Commissioner whether we in Jersey were well up on these data protection issues compared with the UK. Her reply was reassuring: 'We have the huge advantage of being a small jurisdiction. My equivalent in the UK has millions of individuals to consider and hundreds of staff. We on the other hand have a population of, say, 85,000 which is eminently manageable. My small team and I have our fingers on the pulse; I see all the complaints and am very much in touch with the organisations that process data.'

Finally I wanted Emma Martins to tell me whether that early love affair with Jersey was still strong. The answer was a confident one: 'It has never gone. I sometimes have conversations with people who tell me how awful life in the Island is, and a little voice inside me is saying, " Spend a week in Gaza or Zimbabwe or even a deprived area of London or Manchester and then come back and see how you feel". As it is I have a GP five minutes away from me, a dentist whom I can see on the same day and an ambulance ten minutes away if my son were injured. We should rejoice; things can always be better but as a mother I know that my children are as safe as anywhere in the world. There's not a day when I am not grateful.'

And did Emma's father slip back to Jersey sometimes? 'Yes he does come over, but my son is blissfully unaware of how well known his "Papa TV" is. He knows he's on television but has no idea of his fame as they go off rock-pooling together.'

~

I left Morier House and walked up Hill Street, where once the lawyers used to be, and along Colomberie to Grenville Street, home of HSBC Private Bank, Merryll Lynch, Ing Private Banking, Mourant and other institutions. I was making for the Club Hotel, its Bohemia Restaurant and acclaimed chef Shaun Rankin. As it happened, I arrived at the same time as Edward Sault of BBC Channel Islands News, loaded down with his camera and tripod and also with an appointment to meet our chef. This suited me admirably: Shaun came to meet us both, and I moved with Edward and him into the kitchens and sat myself at the chef's table while Shaun was filmed preparing mussels and frogs' legs with the brigade around and behind him very busy (it was 10 a.m.) preparing food for the start of the lunch service at noon. And why was our local television there? Shaun Rankin had recently cooked very successfully on the BBC2 Great British Menu programme which was about to be screened.

Having been interviewed by Edward Sault, Shaun joined me and we sat in Bohemia's bar and chatted. He told me something of his life and career: 'I'm from County Durham and went on to do City and Guilds catering qualifications in Slough. After that I gained experience in the kitchens of some of London's grandest hotels: the Mayfair, the Ritz and the Savoy. I came to Jersey sixteen years ago to work for the Lewis family as sous-chef at Longueville Manor. I was with them nine years and, while taking a year out in Australia, was invited back by the Lewises to launch Suma's restaurant at Gorey. From there I was approached by the Huggler family to open Bohemia; that was six years ago.'

I have eaten and enjoyed marvellous food at Bohemia several times. I wanted Shaun to define what was his style of cookery that won him a Michelin star after only one year. 'It's changed over the years,' he told me. 'My cooking now is very much based on Jersey produce. I like to follow the seasons: the fish, the shellfish, the vegetables. The style is back to basics: great produce cooked very simply; classic dishes with a new twist added. And presentation is also so important: like everything in life, if it doesn't look nice you don't want to sample it.'

With his brigade toiling away at this relatively early hour, I wanted to know just how unsocial his hours of work were. 'We kick off at 8.30 and lunch starts at 12 and finishes at 2.30. I like to get the guys away for a couple of hours then and they are back again at 5, and it's then all the way through to 11 or 12. You just learn to live with the routine, and for me it's a six-day week.'

Bohemia Restaurant

I had heard of chefs in France committing suicide under the strain of seeking Michelin recognition. I now asked Shaun what the Michelin star meant to him. 'Yes, it's a great achievement personally. When you join the cooking ranks, it is what you aspire to. But you lack feed-back from the Michelin people: is your standard one-star or rising two-star and so on? You are somewhat left in this grey area every year.' I wondered whether the Michelin inspectors could be recognised when they arrived in the restaurant. 'No,' said Shaun, 'where we are in St Helier with all these businesses on our doorstep we so often have one or two "ones" eating in the restaurant. You never know.' And Shaun added this: 'The Michelin star is of course important for the hotel and it also encourages staff to come and work for us, those who want to cook at this level.'

I wondered what Shaun Rankin's ambitions now were. Where might he be in ten years' time? His first answer was a prompt one and possibly not accurate: 'Hopefully sitting on a beach with a gin and tonic.' But he does nurse ambitions to have his own business one day: 'I would love to re-create a couple of decent pubs, going back to really simple cooking – Lancashire hotpot, cheese and onion pie, tongue, jellied veal and piccalilli. Bring back really good pub food.' And would he stay in Jersey? 'I have a wife and son here. I'm rather glad I came, and Bohemia has been my big achievement. Might I open up in Jersey? Possibly, but the market is fickle.'

We came to the end of our discussion and for Shaun the kitchen and the lunch service beckoned. Our renowned chef ended with a personal observation: 'I actually got married at Longueville Manor. We had a marquee in the grounds.' 'And,' I asked, 'did they cater well for you?' 'Yes, they did; it was a phenomenal day.'

~

I came out of Bohemia, crossed the road and walked into Green Street Cemetery. It was opened in 1827 and Brett describes it as 'a rather depressing rectangle of grass and grave-stones'. I think that he is being slightly unfair: overgrown cemeteries have a special atmosphere that is unique to them, and this graveyard, despite the proximity of houses, busy roads and a multi-storey car park, does not lack this beguiling quality. In the Michelin guidebook phraseology it is 'worth a detour'. A notice at its entrance calls it 'a green lung for St Helier', stating that a hundred species of plant grow wild here, and goes on to direct one to the impressive Le Cronier Monument at the cemetery's southern end. I strolled its length to inspect this impressive and diverting structure, twenty-five feet high and in the form of a little Doric temple with a pyramidal roof enclosing a draped urn on a high plinth. What on earth was this all about? One of its inscriptions has this announcement:

> SES CONCITOYENS
> VOULANT PERPETUER LEURS REGRETS
> ET LE SOUVENIR DE SON DEVOUEMENT
> ONT FAIT ERIGER CE MONUMENT
> SUR SES RESTES MORTELS
>
> NE
> LE 30 MARS 1793
> DECEDE LE 28 FEVRIER 1846

It seems that Centenier George Le Cronier, exercising his parochial responsibilities, called at a cottage in Patriotic Street to arrest Marie Le Gendre and her husband for keeping a house of ill-repute. Marie's husband was out; she took up a carving knife and plunged it into the Centenier's stomach; Le Cronier died the following day. The monument is therefore a memorial to this attempt by Virtue to triumph over Vice.

~ THE ROYAL SQUARE TO VICTORIA COLLEGE...

Green Street Cemetery

~

I now walked along Green Street and Francis Street into Don Road. This is part of St Helier's ring road system and traffic comes at a pace off St Saviour's Road and on to the traffic lights at the junction with Mont Millais. I suspect that few drivers notice in Don Road that they are sweeping past two rather fine and tall terraces known as Royal Crescent. They were built in 1828 and the name is a corruption of 'Theatre Royal Crescent'. The Theatre Royal that formed the terraces' centrepiece was burned down in 1863 and its replacement, the New Bible Christian Church, was demolished in 1969 leaving an unappealing space now used as a car park. But the Crescent deserves attention: each of its two terraces consists of nine three-bay three-storey houses constructed on a slight and elegant curve. H.D. Inglis in his book *The Channel Islands* published in 1834 says this about the Royal Crescent: '[It is] inhabited chiefly by the English; it is considerably improved in its appearance by the Theatre which forms the centre of the arch, and whose pretty Greek portico is an agreeable relief to the plainness of the buildings that flank it'. Sadly the Crescent is not as it originally was.

Don Terrace

This is a part of St Helier rich in late Georgian, Regency and early Victorian terraces and villas. Don Terrace, built around 1850 and with its tall stucco semi-detached villas, at the eastern end of Royal Crescent is such an example. A walk up Clarence Road brings one to Grosvenor Street and its terrace built in 1826 and described by Brett as 'a very plain, but on the whole rather magnificent, long large terrace of stucco houses; fifteen houses, no less than forty-five bays in all'.

~

But just before I reached Grosvenor Street I had a call to make at an equally impressive building but of our own time – Jersey Archive, nestling in an old quarry and an example of modern architecture at its thrilling best. Its design was the responsibility of local firm BDK Architects working in association with

London-based MacCormac Jamieson Prichard which had experience of archive and library design elsewhere. Denise Williams, former Head of Archives, has written extensively in the *Journal of The Society of Archivists* about the building and deserves to be quoted:

> The style of the Jersey Archive is very simple and modern. In fact, the contemporary feel of the building is almost startling in Jersey where architectural style is strongly influenced by strict planning laws and the inheritance of the past...The archive building, in an early nineteenth century street, is set back from the road in its quarry so that it does not jar on the eye as one looks from the street...The modern style challenges the often-held misconception that archive buildings should reflect the age of their contents...Jersey's Archive was not to be another symbol of government and the establishment but a place for ordinary people, welcoming, not overwhelming; a place of accessibility, education and pleasure.

Jersey Archive is thus well worth a visit, and I called in to meet Linda Romeril, its current Head of Archives and Collections for Jersey Heritage (to give her full title). 'Yes,' she explained, 'we are part of Jersey Heritage and its Director, Jon Carter, is my direct line manager. I have a dual remit, and the collection side of my job involves responsibility for the Jersey Museum collections as well.' Linda is a Jerseywoman, educated at Hautlieu and then going on to the University of York to read History and English. (I spent the last ten years of my professional life in York and Linda and I discovered that we had a mutual acquaintance in the tutor for her third year medieval history project.) She then took a Master's degree in Archive Administration at the University of Wales in Aberystwyth, coming back to Jersey in 1997, gaining a post at Jersey Archive and becoming its Head of Archives in 2007.

We chatted about the building itself and I asked Linda whether it fulfilled all the hopes of its designers. Her answer was unsurprisingly in the affirmative: 'Yes, it is pretty well spot on. Last year a survey was done of UK archives and we scored in the top five per cent.' I also learned something of Jersey's archival history or lack of it: 'We had no archive service before 1993. Previously records were kept all over the place – basements, cellars, attics – and a lot of material was in very poor condition. One of the triggers changing all this was the theft of important Occupation documents. Fortunately most of the papers were retrieved, but this sparked off the realisation that new facilities were needed. The Archive was initially housed at No.9 Pier Road, but in 1997 the funding for this new facility was provided. The problem is now of course the running costs and this has to come from Jersey Heritage's tight budget. That is why we are currently open to the public for only three days a week; we just don't have the staff to open more often.'

Jersey Archive

I wondered whether the Archive would ever run out of space. 'If people keep producing paper,' replied Linda, 'then that could be so many years hence. But it is my job to identify what is archive material from States departments, and a complication these days is that so much information is now electronic.' And the number of users? 'Last year we were open for 160 days and had just over 3,500 people here. If we get over thirty visitors a day, then we are fairly well up to capacity.' And what were the main interests of visitors? 'It is genealogy mostly

– people doing family history and researching into the history of their property. And we have a growing number of visitors here for professional reasons – lawyers researching precedents for cases and engineering firms and architects consulting maps and plans. Then there are Jersey university students who have decided to do their dissertations on the Island's history. We also work with the schools: we go out to them and they come to us.'

I next asked Linda Romeril whether she had any big objectives for the future. 'Our main ambition,' she replied, 'is obviously to be open more, to give the public greater access. We would also love to do more with school children – from the young up to A-level students. We must also work with States departments on their modern records, making sure that the right information is kept to ensure government accountability and that there are no black holes for future researchers. Looking after these burgeoning electronic records is a major challenge, a really key area for the whole archive profession.'

Finally Jersey's Head of Archives spoke of her eight members of staff and the huge enthusiasm they have for their work. And her own enthusiasm is palpable: 'I am incredibly lucky to have landed this job; fantastic.' On that very happy note we rose from her office and I was given a guided tour of this fine and striking facility. I entered the strong room with massive on-rail metal shelving, temperature-controlled and on four floors, and visited the areas for conservation and cataloguing. The Island deserves to be proud of its Archive, its striking appearance, its comprehensive facilities and its important function in the life of the community.

~

I left Jersey Archive, headed north up Pleasant Street and joined St Saviour's Road. Here on the right was the Le Bas Centre, formerly Jersey's maternity hospital. I was interested to walk across its threshold once again since this was where in 1975 and again in 1976 I had done sentry duty in the labour ward for many hours when my son and daughter were born. (I recall that on the first of these two occasions I was attempting to read Richard Crossman's Cabinet diaries when not occupied in wiping my wife's brow.) This time I had no need of a book and my visit was somewhat more brief; I was on my way to meet Jersey's Medical Officer of Health, Dr Rosemary Geller. I first of all learned something of Dr Geller's early life and career: brought up in Shropshire, educated in the sixth form at Epsom College, with medical training at Birmingham University Medical School and then a career in public health medicine. She told me more: 'After specialist training in Birmingham I held public health posts in Solihull and then in Shropshire before becoming Director of Health Strategy and Public Health for Shropshire and Staffordshire Health Authority. In 2005 this post in Jersey came up where as

Medical Officer of Health/Director of Public Health I am medical adviser to the States.' Rosemary told me that she knew Jersey well from a young age: 'I visited on holiday with my parents when I was a child; after I married, my husband and I came to the Island with friends; and then later we had family holidays here with our two daughters. There is so much that I love about Jersey.'

I wanted our Medical Officer of Health to take the temperature for me of the Island's health. Did we compare well with elsewhere? With some qualifications Rosemary's response was reassuring: 'We are "good average" in terms of our general health, but we are not world leaders such as Japan, Switzerland and Canada. France too is almost up there. So this is my aspiration: that Jersey should not only be a world-leading economy but also a world-leading jurisdiction for good health.' And what were particular issues, I asked. 'High alcohol consumption is one of them; it is higher than that of Glasgow. And then there are raised rates of head, neck and lung cancer; these are related to past levels of smoking which are now falling nicely. One of my daily duties is to sign cremation forms, and this gives me an insight into a group of younger people dying mostly from diseases related to smoking and alcohol; for me a reminder every day of what is wrong and where we could do better. Then obesity is yet another problem: too much and the wrong sort of food and this is compounded by the lack of exercise taken by people today compared with the past where physical exercise just happened naturally in the course of living.'

Dr Geller then discussed with me the difficulty at times of getting her message across. She said more: 'It is commonly thought that if you smoke and drink too much this is your own choice. But it is more complex than that and to do with society; if children see others drinking and smoking all around them, then they themselves are more likely to over-indulge. Also Jersey has twice as many licensed establishments to sell or serve alcohol than is the case in the UK. And research studies tell us this: if you have twice as many licensed premises, you sell more alcohol.'

Then how does our Medical Officer of Health tackle these issues? 'I do this in a number of ways, and the biggest opportunity is through influencing the States; their actions and their funding can make Jersey a different and healthier place. I dislike the term "nanny state"; I believe that is the accusation thrown out by those who have a financial interest such as the tobacco industry which makes money whilst others die young. And I have no difficulty in trying to persuade and advise individuals in order for them to live long and healthy lives. It is important for me to attempt to give leadership here, and it is helpful that my Annual Report goes to all States Members and that the media are always interested and give it generous coverage.'

I was told of one other big medical problem for which Jersey seems well prepared: the big challenge of a flu pandemic. 'I do believe,' said Dr Geller, 'that it is a major risk and we are prepared for it. We are stockpiling a vaccine based on the bird flu variety, and it would be available for all Islanders. So we are fortunately ahead of the game compared with the UK: not only a supply for healthcare workers but enough for the whole population. (I was talking to the Medical Officer of Health just weeks before any of us had heard of swine flu.)

Reassured as far as any paid-up hypochondriac could be, I turned finally to more general matters. Rosemary Geller relishes living with her family in Jersey – the scenery, the cliff walks, the green lanes, the restaurants, the wonderful environment in which to bring up children. But the one thing that disappointed her when coming permanently to the Island was the traffic. She added this: 'We need a better transport infrastructure, especially for walking and cycling. It is a nightmare in St Helier where more pedestrianisation would surely be of benefit. Yes, it is a challenge for an island with limited space, but go to any German or Dutch city and see their wide pavements and cycle tracks. You know, there's a correlation between well-planned towns that promote physical activity and good health. Here in Jersey it would require a big injection of capital to change people's travel habits for the better.'

~

I left the Le Bas Centre and the welcoming and informative Dr Geller and returned to St Saviour's Road with its rush of transport and its confusing traffic lanes and walked safely a few yards along the pavement to a venue that was new to me, Jersey's Animals' Shelter. The Chief Executive Officer of JSPCA/Animals' Shelter (his full title) is Major Stephen Coleman and, as with most of my interviewees, I first sought something of his background history. Stephen is a retired Army officer, commissioned into the Devon and Dorset Regiment in 1974, with a degree from the Royal Military College of Science and service both in the Falklands and (numerous times) in Northern Ireland. He is a 'local boy' who was running Sky's operation in the Channel Islands when he secured his present post in 2006. His was an initiation of fire and he gave me some details: 'I was appointed at the back of an *annus horribilis* for the organisation. There had been a number of allegations levelled at the Society and I was appointed as a new broom. In my first week I had the Director-General of Battersea Dogs' Home carrying out a cruelty investigation and a banking regulator doing a financial audit. Donations were down and we were struggling. Fortunately we are now in a much healthier state: a good solid financial reserve and keeping our profile high with my weekly slot on BBC local radio and our re-homing page in the *JEP*.'

Stephen then told me more: 'The JSPCA was incorporated as an animal anti-cruelty organisation as far back as 1863, and the Animals' Shelter here goes back to 1912 when our founder Frances Wilson bought this place in 1912. It was in fact a working farm and continued as such until the late 1930s. And the two separate organisations came together by an act of the States in 1936.' The Shelter's history during the Occupation was intriguing; Stephen filled me in: 'Our work continued during that time. Now part of our constitution provides for free euthanasia and, prior to embarkation in 1940 just before the Germans arrived, 1000 animals a day were brought here for a week to be put down; a gruesome and sad fact. Once the Germans were here our committee decided on a pet food-rationing scheme. The Germans thought this absolutely right, and animal carcasses not fit for human consumption were collected from the slaughterhouse, cooked and the meat then distributed to pet owners.'

We now got on to less squeamish territory with Major Coleman telling me about the core activities of the Animals' Shelter and his twenty full-time and fourteen part-time staff. They include the 24-hour animal ambulance provision for strays and injured animals, the boarding facility that produces useful income for the Society, the pet crematorium, a cruelty and investigation service used by the States, re-homing (new and loving homes for unwanted animals) and the free welfare clinic available to pet owners on income support. I asked how many dogs and cats brought into the Shelter had to be put down. Stephen replied: 'Since 2006 we have re-homed any animal that was suitable. Our longest resident was here eighteen months and then we found a home for him. The fact is that we manage to re-home them all except for the few unsuitable ones that would be a danger.'

And funding for all this fine activity and service? 'We have a number of core activities that generate income; cremation and boarding are two of our main sources. Then our services to States departments attract a fee. After that it is up to me to raise the profile and attract donations. We do very well in this area. You see, it costs us £18,000 a week to keep the Shelter and the service we offer going.'

I wondered whether Stephen could give me a head count of this day's residents. Yes, he could: 'We have eleven resident dogs; we have twenty-two cats looking for homes; and there are eighteen cats and twelve rabbits in our clinic (they have a fortnight in our hospital suite before they go to our re-homing facility). So there are twenty rabbits looking for a home as well as six hamsters, fifteen chinchillas and one mouse.'

After receipt of this remarkable statistic, not least the last part of it, I was given a very comprehensive tour of the campus: the operating theatre, the dogs' re-homing kennels, the cattery, the boarding kennels, the quarantine areas, the rooms for treating oil-infected sea birds, the provision for snakes and other reptiles, the enclosed exercise yard (rather like a prison facility!) and the nature trail at the top of the property that stretches up the side of the hill from St Saviour's Road to Mont Millais. I departed the Animals' Shelter a wiser man, leaving behind much bustle and activity and quite a lot of barking.

~ THE ROYAL SQUARE TO VICTORIA COLLEGE...

~

I now cheated just a little and took a tentative step into the parish of St Saviour. A little further along St Saviour's Road, past the Wellington Road junction, is the Hotel de France and in front of it the building which was previously Kevin Lewis's Cinécentre. Reconstruction a few years back has transformed it into the Lido Medical Centre. I entered and took the lift (another extremely swish example) up to the third floor and the rooms of Dr Ng, Jersey's consultant gastroenterologist. I sat for a short while in the ultra-smart reception area chatting with his private practice secretary about this and that. I suggested to her that I would not detain Dr Ng for too long. She replied that there would be no problem since he was a man of few words. He then called me in to his consulting room where we sat and conversed freely for at least half an hour. It transpired in our discussion that his secretary outside was none other than his wife. I then blurted out that she had just told me that he had no small talk. 'Don't worry,' was his jovial reply; 'she's always teasing me.'

David Ng was born in Liverpool. His father was from Hong Kong and his mother from mainland China, and in England their business was first a Chinese laundry and then fish and chips. 'I come from quite a humble background, passed the 11-plus and went to Prescot Grammar School. I was fortunate in gaining entry to Liverpool Medical School and graduated from there in 1985.' And what brought him into this particular medical specialty? 'It was providence really: the first consultant for whom I worked was a gastroenterologist and it was he that mentored me through my early career. I did research in Nottingham, was a senior registrar in Manchester and then a consultant in Lincoln for eight years before coming to Jersey in 2003.'

And why Jersey? 'I had met Jersey's gastroenterologist at a conference and he told me that he was retiring at the end of the year. I had never been to Jersey before, so I brought the family over to visit the Island and the hospital, and everyone was delightful and friendly. We stayed at L'Horizon in St Brelade's Bay with a sea-front room and, when we woke up and looked out, my wife was sold on the idea of coming and encouraged me to apply for the post.'

I then asked Dr Ng to explain in simple terms what gastroenterology was. He obliged: 'It is the study of the gastrointestinal tract – from where one swallows to where it passes out. It also includes hepatology which is the study of liver disease and pancreatology, the study of disease of the pancreas. Basically it is concerned with that hollow tube which runs through the middle of the body and the various disorders that can occur – from inherited disorder to age-related disorder. With the diseases of the liver and pancreas, these may be from a number of causes such as infection or alcoholism. It's a fairly broad field of medical expertise.'

With some of Dr Geller's comments in mind, I wondered whether David Ng had encountered any particular Jersey problems in his specialist field. His reply was possibly reassuring: 'Before I arrived I was told that Jersey consisted of 90,000 alcoholics clinging to a rock. But I have actually found that alcohol is not such a major problem; people here do drink slightly more than normal but not excessively to the point where they are socially disabled or physically compromised. It is of course important to give recommendations and advice concerning the use of alcohol but there is not a problem special to Jersey.'

My next question concerned the difference between working for the NHS in England and practising here. A strong response followed: 'Oh yes, it has been a breath of fresh air coming to Jersey. The big plus is less central control; I am a single-handed consultant in my specialty and thus have more influence on how the service develops. I can be more responsive to requirements without the slow grind of NHS bureaucracy. When I came I recognised that there were improvements to be made and within six months I had been able to update equipment and get the nursing staff that were needed. This sort of thing took far longer in my previous post in Lincoln.

Dr Ng and I then discussed Jersey and private medicine. He told me that, with medical insurance being a perk for many in the finance industry and also for some States employees, thirty-five per cent of Jersey's population had private cover. He added this: 'The unusual thing about Jersey private procedures is that they have to be performed in the General Hospital. But, while I therefore have to mix my private with my public work, this arrangement does provide income worth several million pounds a year for the States. With a private hospital that money would go elsewhere.'

Finally I invited David Ng after his five years in the Island to tell me how he viewed Jersey. 'The patients,' he replied, 'are lovely – well educated and generally health-aware. Perhaps they don't always realise how good is our hospital when compared with the NHS – cleaner, better food, a more generous nurse/patient ratio and expert consultants. The Island is a small community and we must be particularly careful about the quality of the service we give.' And David added a further factor: 'I haven't got a great memory for names and faces and it can be awkward when someone comes up and says, "Do you remember me, Dr Ng. You did that colonoscopy on me two years ago." It can sometimes be a bit inhibiting trying to be anonymous.' I suggested in reply to this that surely it was less the faces of his patients that he saw but rather the other end. Dr Ng gave a chuckle and told me that at least he saw their faces first.

And a final thought? 'Jersey perhaps takes a little time to get used to, to settle in. But we are very happy here, with our daughter up the hill at Beaulieu Convent School.' Indeed, back to Wellington Road, a return to the parish of St Helier and up the hill to Beaulieu: that was precisely where I was heading.

~

Schools were my way of life for thirty-five years until my retirement from teaching and then headships. Walking from Wellington Road up the driveway to Beaulieu Convent School was thus not the approach to an unfamiliar environment. It must have been a lesson change when I arrived, with large numbers of girls going in one direction and another as I reported in at the reception desk and was then warmly welcomed by Chris Beirne, headmaster since 2004. We sat in his ordered and attractive study (with a very uncluttered desk; always a good sign) and chatted for an hour. I learned that he has very strong Irish roots with a father originally from the West who set up a pharmacy business in Northamptonshire. Chris nonetheless, after prep school in England, had his secondary education as a boarder at his father's old school, the Jesuit St Mel's College in County Longford where he had, in his words, 'a tremendous time', ended up as Head Boy and gained a valued lesson in what good quality Catholic schools are able to offer.

He went on to tell me what happened next: 'I first thought of pharmacy as a career but decided to explore my vocation for the priesthood. What then followed were seven years at the Venerable English College in Rome, degrees in Philosophy and Theology at the Gregorian University there, a six-month placement in the English section of the Vatican Secretariat of State and ordination into the diaconate. A year later I was priested in the Northampton diocese and then spent a short time as a curate in Milton Keynes and Kettering after which I became personal secretary to the Bishop of Northampton. After three years in that post I was invited to go back to Rome and take up a position in the Vatican Congregation for Catholic Education. I saw beckoning a lifestyle with which I did not feel completely comfortable; perhaps God was telling me that I could contribute in other ways than through ministry. And I sought laicisation – the process for a priest to apply to be relieved of his duties and revert to the lay state. I had to wait until I was forty and this was then granted.'

Chris then told me how at this stage he moved into teaching, first Religious Education at a school in Hampshire and then after three years, having just married, coming in 1995 to Jersey as Victoria College's Head of Divinity. He was three years there and then moved across the road to be Deputy Head of Jersey College for Girls. He was eight years at JCG, with a total of a year and a half when he was holding the fort during interregnums between heads. And then came another move of no more than a few hundred yards with his appointment as the first headmaster of Beaulieu.

Why the name Beaulieu? Chris Beirne gave me the history: 'The school started here in 1951 when this large house, built in 1824 and called Beaulieu, was purchased by the Sisters of the Immaculate Conception. At the time there were fifty pupils; nearly six decades on we have 200 in our primary department and 570 in the senior school and that includes 130 in the sixth form. In the early days all the teaching was done by the nuns but there are no Sisters now. I am only the fourth head, and the second one was Sister Marie Louise. She is Patron of our Foundation and one of our Trustees, a wonderful character who sees her ministry now as being to pray for Beaulieu. I refer to her as the Holy Spirit that walks through the school. She is part of that tradition which is so special in a school such as this.'

There is no doubt that Beaulieu is flourishing under its first headmaster's guidance. Chris was able to tell me how oversubscribed it was, with credit crunches and financial difficulties seeming to have little effect on a very healthy level of applications. Unlike Victoria College and JCG, Beaulieu is independent of the States and this gives Chris a degree of confidence in his dealings with the States education department (which does, it has to be said, give financial help that subsidises this independent school's fees though not making any contribution to its capital developments).

Chris Beirne's energies are directed to maintaining that special ethos deriving from the presence over the years of the Sisters, 'giving breadth and opportunity and challenge to our students and enhancing the values and traditions of the school'. He added this: 'We work within restrained resources to deliver a quality education. It took me a period of time, prayer, reflection and judgment to build up our key team, giving them confidence to deliver. I am convinced that the product we have at Beaulieu is moving towards gold standard, and I am not going to let that out of my grasp.'

Before I left Beaulieu I was privileged to be given a tour of the school by its headmaster. Carpeted corridors, classrooms, the library (where I was flattered to be invited to sign two of my previous books), art department, sports areas, laboratories, quiet chapel, all looked in fine and familiar shape to this retired eye. I was even taken into what was once the ballroom of the original house and told that it was here that Queen Victoria was reputed to have danced when she came to open her eponymous College some yards away. I could hardly argue with my headmaster host, but Balleine in his *A History of the Island of Jersey* describes only two visits of Her Majesty to the Island, the first being for three hours in 1846, six years before the College was built, and then a shorter and surprise visit in 1859 when there seemed to have been no time at all for dancing. It is though a nice story and I hope that Chris Beirne makes sure that he tells it to all prospective parents when he gives them his tour of the school. For me he had been an admirable host and more than generous with his time and attention.

~

Before I moved on in the direction of Victoria College I had the opportunity of a chat with Beaulieu's Head Girl, Naomi Garton. Naomi told me that she was born in Jersey and that her parents had come over from England and were both teachers. 'Indeed,' she added, 'my mother is on the staff here at Beaulieu. Yes, it was a bit awkward when she taught me in Year 7 and I also had her for my German GCSE. But it's a different relationship and I wouldn't call her "Mum" in class!' Naomi was now coming up to her A-levels in History, English Literature and French and had offers from Exeter University and King's College, London, to read Law and French Law.

I wondered what Naomi's interests were outside school. 'I used to do a lot of horse-riding,' she replied, 'but then I had to get a Saturday job working in a pharmacy. I do a lot of running. And I had a holiday work expcrience post at Mourant last summer as a legal assistant; good for my university application form.' And what, I asked Beaulieu's Head Girl, was the essence of the school? 'For me it has been the sense of community, everyone pulling together and the support from the teachers. It's a very friendly place and the staff are brilliant. I've always been very happy here.'

My next question was this: what did Jersey mean to her? Naomi's response was unsurprisingly positive: 'I'm incredibly lucky. We live just behind St Ouen's Bay at Grantez, and one can stroll towards the sea – one of my favourite views in all the world. And yes, there are times, more in the winter perhaps, when it is a tiny bit frustrating and there is that itch to get away. So for me Jersey is very beautiful but a tad constricting. Let's call it a "constrictive paradise".'

I then wondered whether she and her contemporaries took any interest in the Island's political affairs. Did Beaulieu sixth formers in their common room chat about the States and what went on there? 'I'm afraid we don't. The political scene is perhaps rather male-dominated and not terribly attractive. But I did vote at the last States election.' And a final thought? 'I would never have wanted to grow up anywhere else other than Jersey, nor would I have ever wanted to go to a school other than this one.'

~

I now took the lane that leads from Beaulieu to the entrance gates of Victoria College. Here I must declare an interest in that I was privileged to be a member of its Board of Governors for seven years. Architecturally the College receives generous treatment in Brett's *Buildings in the Town and Parish of St Helier*, more so than any other group in the parish. The school's main building dates from 1852, is clearly visible from various locations in the town and is described in these terms by Brett: 'A tall, symmetrical, rather heavy-handed Gothic Revival building…disappointing from close up but really rather fine when seen from below, and from a distance, on the summit of its steeply sloping site'. Upstairs is the impressive school hall with its hammerbeam roof, its honours boards and its large Winterhalter paintings (or are they copies?) of Victoria and Albert. And if a youth were summoned to the headmaster's study, then he would be required to visit the delightful former summerhouse, built in 1810 in the style of a Doric temple, the last remnant of the estate that was here before the College.

Having spoken with Beaulieu's Head Girl, I was also anxious to have a chat with the Head Boy of Victoria College, and Callum Gillies was not a total stranger. He lives two hundred yards away from us in St Mary and a decade or so ago I would see him and his mother, plus marvellously obedient border collie (with a little other added), coming up our lane in the mornings on their way to St Mary's primary school. Here now was Callum, having almost completed his seven years at Vic., studying for his A-levels in Physics, Chemistry, Biology, Maths and Further Maths and hoping to take up a university place to read Medical Physics which, he told me, was the study of imaging techniques and engineering related to medicine and biology.

I wonder whether Callum's surname rings any bells with older Jersey residents? He is the son of Stuart Gillies who entertained so many of the Island's holiday visitors especially at Grève de Lecq's Caesar's Palace in the heyday of Jersey's tourist industry. Stuart, Callum told me, still sings as a guest entertainer on cruise ships, and the spin-off for this has been Callum's sixteen or so cruises with father and family round much of the world. When on these trips did he go, I asked, to Dad's on-board shows? Callum's reply was explanatory: 'If I go to one, that keeps him happy.'

Callum follows in the family's musical traditions (his mother teaches dance): he is a singer (a lead part in *Les Misérables* not so long ago and member of a barbershop group), dancer, drummer and guitarist. He has a Saturday job at Fort Regent teaching younger children singing and a holiday job at St Mary's Community Centre with its kids' club. Add to that occasional tasks at the Opera House, involvement with Performance, a company that offers stilt-walking, dressing up and corporate gigs, and freelance work with the company that provides for Jersey Live. The list continues: he has been a second row forward in the College rugger team and a corporal in its award-winning Combined Cadet Force. He is a busy fellow!

Almost out of breath myself, I got on to asking Callum about Victoria College: what had been his first impressions when he joined the school at the age of eleven? 'I was almost overwhelmed,' he replied, 'coming from rural St Mary's. Here was this massive Hogswartesque building: the Great Hall, the traditions, the gowned prefects, the ethos of the place. And I have remained impressed. The school has a fantastic staff, and possibly its being all-boy keeps the distractions at bay. And the resources are so good: the sixth form centre is brilliant; the learning resources centre has just been renovated.'

~ THE ROYAL SQUARE TO VICTORIA COLLEGE...

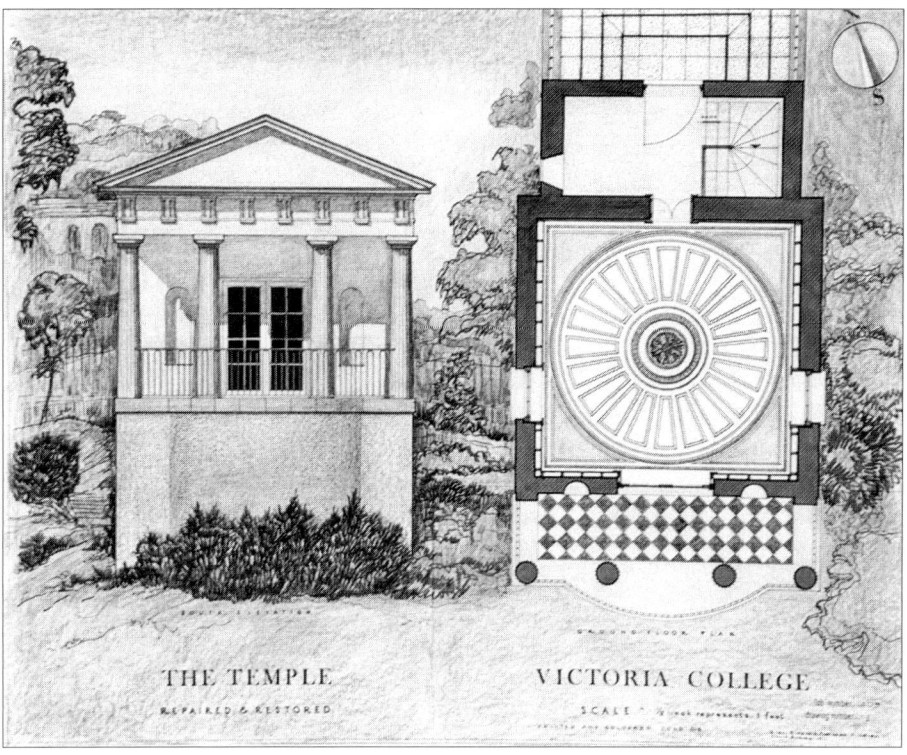

As with Naomi Garton at the school almost next door, I wanted to know Callum's thoughts about Jersey where he was born and educated. He replied: 'I have always loved the Island. When occasionally I have been in England I hanker for St Mary, the countryside and the town. It's a shame what has happened to our tourist industry and the entertainments that went with it. My dad, for instance, couldn't make a job here any more. Indeed he thinks that we should encourage the cruise ships here and bring in the passengers on tenders as is done elsewhere.'

And political interest in Jersey's affairs? 'Well, I voted in the last elections and there was much discussion about it all in the common room. Possibly a quarter to a half of our over-sixteens did go to the polls. For myself I don't have a great deal of time to investigate the political issues but I try and keep up. It's important to do so. One of the big challenges facing Jersey is this business of young people going off to university and not coming back. Problems of accommodation and the price of property is a factor here. But Jersey in one word? Fantastic.'

6

The Royal Square to Fort Regent by way of Commercial Buildings, La Collette and Havre des Pas

Before my final stroll round St Helier, I sat in the warm sunshine outside the Cock and Bottle in the Royal Square and chatted with one of our newest and youngest States Members, Deputy Montfort Tadier. He had emerged from a morning session in the States Chamber and was anticipating a long afternoon on his return to its benches. Over orange juice for him, mineral water for me and salads for both of us I was able to discover why this young Jerseyman had turned to politics and what he hoped to achieve from this new and challenging change in his life.

My first question, with thoughts of Simon de Montfort and the summoning of the first English Parliament in mind, concerned his first name, and Deputy Tadier, born in 1979, told me that his mother was French and that she had known of a saint with the 'de Montfort' tag. From a family with a religious background, he had at school – Les Quennevais and then Hautlieu – decided to specialise in languages and then gone on to Sheffield University for his degree in French and German. His studies had taken him to both Réunion in the Indian Ocean and Martinique before his returning to Jersey and a three-year spell working for Jersey Telecom. Besides his current duties as a States Deputy he told me that he did translation work, an occupation that ticked along mainly by e-mail and hence allowed him to devote himself fully to his political activities.

How long, I asked Montfort Tadier, had he been a political animal? 'It had always been in the back of my mind,' he replied. 'At the age of 18 and at school we each completed a yearbook stating our plans for the future. I wrote that I would go away, become a famous linguist and then come back to Jersey and stand for the States. Well, perhaps the first objective didn't quite come off, but the second has.' He continued: 'I've always been interested in politics and even at the age of 13 or 14 I had bought into the whole Jersey ideology – Jersey a successful place, the importance of protecting the finance industry and so on. My years abroad perhaps effected some sort of change in my perspectives. And there's a

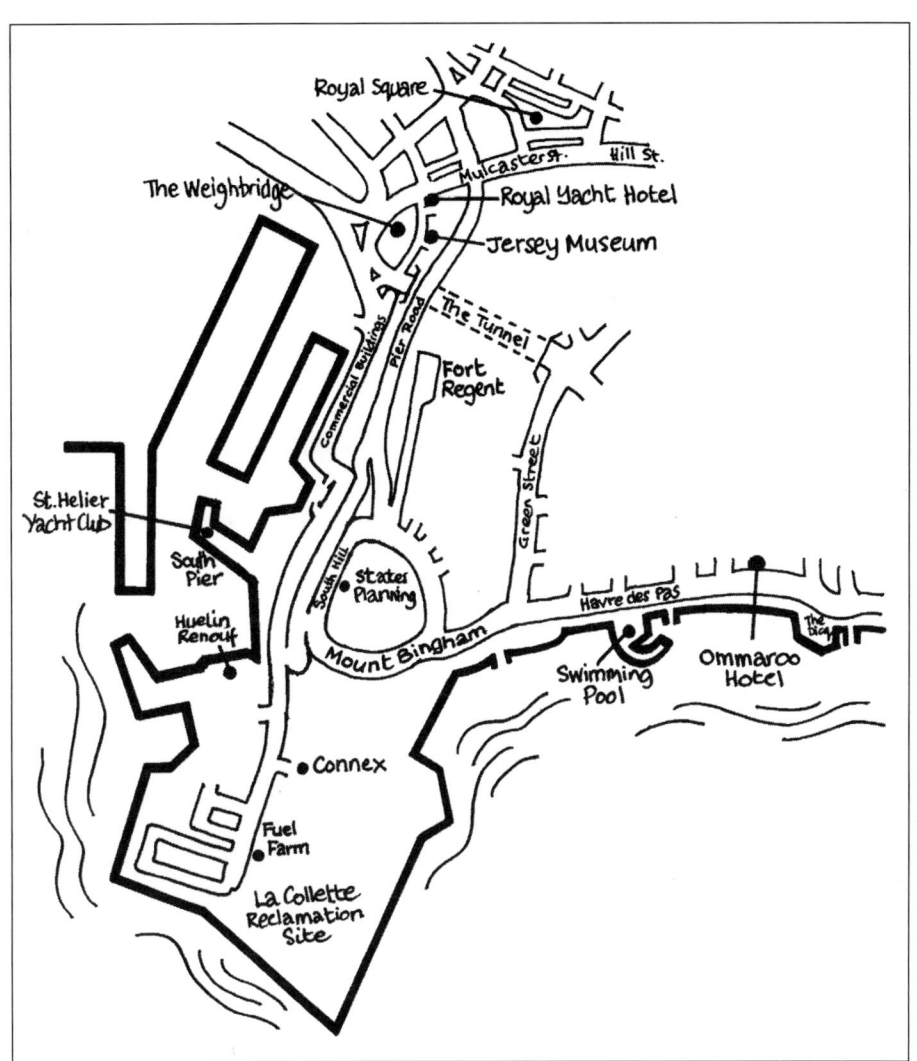

proud tradition in Jersey of kicking the establishment: people possibly holding the contradictory views of being something of a maverick while at the same time at heart a conservative and knowing that, while having a go at the establishment, nothing is likely to change. It's a kind of safe position that some take up.'

Montfort had originally flirted with the newly launched Jersey Democratic Alliance but was now no longer a member. Where, I asked him, was he on the Jersey political spectrum? 'Perhaps I am a bit to the left, but remember that in the Island's government there are left-wingers who would be termed Conservatives elsewhere.' And his political objectives, his reasons for standing for the States? 'I stood on a reform ticket. I am involved with an informal coalition of States Members whose main thrust is to do with reforming the States and making it human rights compliant. Take for instance the conflicting judiciary/legislature roles – the positions for example of the Bailiff and the Attorney General in the States. These arrangements are now under scrutiny.'

We then discussed the proposals of the Clothier Commission which recommended radical changes to Jersey's machinery of government, the States and the electoral system almost a decade ago. Montfort's comments were clear: 'Clothier should have been adopted and part of my political function is to chip away at these as yet unreformed Jersey practices. I am on the States committee putting forward proposals for change and I support the ending of the position of Senators and the reform of electoral districts. The issue of the Constables in the States is a key issue; I am a pragmatist about this one but would one day favour a radical solution for their removal.'

Was our young and new Deputy an optimist or pessimist concerning the Island's future? 'We live in precarious times both politically and economically. For Jersey it could be business as usual in the years ahead, but we also require an insurance plan. Diversification is ultimately what we need; there is the possibility that finance may decline (and there are the moral questions about the finance industry to be asked and its implications for the rest of the world, and this is a subject on which most States Members are conspicuously silent). Finance may not leave overnight; and yet it could happen very quickly, and then Jersey would be in real trouble. There is a lack of vision about this in the States; I once asked the Chief Minister whether there was a Plan B if finance were to leave. His reply was, 'No; we must ensure finance's future."

And a final thought from Deputy Tadier before he returned to his seat in the States Chamber? 'It is even more pronounced in Jersey than in other places that change takes a long time to bring off. Public opinion shifts and yet it is not represented in the States or only years later. The truth is this: if you can't get the basics of democracy right, then you are likely to get everything else wrong – because there is no true representation.' With that firm statement one of the Island's youngest politicians took his leave of me, he to the heat of the States

Chamber and I, in perhaps a more temperate atmosphere, to my final journey round the Island's capital.

Royal Square

~

I left the Royal Square and all its associations with Jersey's judicial and political arrangements, passed the Town Church and proceeded down the somewhat dull Mulcaster Street to the Weighbridge where major work was currently in progress to turn the unsightly and unlamented bus station into a notable piazza. Bordering this to-be-welcomed open space is the Royal Yacht Hotel, the original part of it a hostelry for 150 years, and its flashy, exciting, brand-new extension, which will surely complement the burgeoning development in front of it. I dropped in to have a chat with the hotel's manager, Alcino Vieira, and we sat at a table in the smart, ground-floor café, as he told me something of his long Jersey career. He came to the Island in 1974, worked at the Somerville Hotel and then at Sea Crest before moving into management, first at Winston's on the Five Mile Road, later at La Haule Manor and then for the company owning the Royal Yacht since 1992. He told me how he and I were actually sitting on the site of the former bus garage and how he had convinced his directors of the potential in purchasing it. 'Eventually,' he added, 'it all transpired and we now have a magnificent 110-room world-class hotel that opened in July 2006. The architects were the local firm of

Naish Waddington; it is privately owned by the Taylor family and this was the biggest private investment ever in the Channel Islands - £30m.' I asked Mr Vieira what customers they were aiming to attract and in reply he spoke of the important corporate business and also the hotel's tourist appeal as well as its immediate popularity with local people, mentioning especially the Sunday lunchtime buffets crowded with Jersey families. 'For example there is the fine dining upstairs in the Restaurant Sirocco and next door there's the lively atmosphere of the bar; something for everyone.' I wondered about the competition from the newly opened Radisson on the waterfront. The manager's response was quick: 'There's room for both, absolutely. Competition is healthy for us. That is good. We have our market and they theirs.' When I asked him about Jersey's tourism he pointed out that it was no longer like the old days when getting to Jersey was so cheap. 'We are attracting a different, more demanding and discerning clientele, and that's good for Jersey, and the Royal Yacht is here to meet that demand.' Alcino Vieira, with his new luxury hotel to manage seems a fulfilled and happy man, looking forward to the work outside being completed. 'It will be better than 30 buses pulling in and out. The only trouble was the timing: we got our building job finished first.'

As I left I caught up with two of the Royal Yacht's staff in the hotel foyer. Carlos Mogueira was the smart porter on duty. He has been in Jersey for six years, spending a year or so at Les Quennevais School before looking for employment and then working for the Royal Yacht since its opening. He told me that his parents had been in the Island for 20 years. Would Jersey be his home for evermore? 'I am not sure yet, but I am very happy working here at the hotel. That goes for everyone. It is all really nice.'

Behind the impressive hotel desk was Ovalerie Wendiady, originally from Indonesia, who has been working in Jersey for three years and is head receptionist at the Royal Yacht. She has a degree in management and has previously worked in Los Angeles and in Birmingham. She told me about her job: 'I have been here since before we opened. It's been challenging and a lot of fun, and I am responsible for the smooth running of the front of house operations.' She likes Jersey especially for its island style of life: 'I admire the traditional aspects of it, for instance the sense that Sunday is a family day, that those who live here have a pride and a sense of community.' And she gave me a slick profile of the hotel's guests: 'From Mondays to Thursdays it is predominantly business; from Fridays to Sundays we cater more for leisure guests and the locals, with the Sunday brunch being particularly popular with families.' I made a mental note to return for food and sustenance as I stepped out from this new, glittering example of Jersey's hospitality industry.

~

It was only a step next door to the Museum and the offices of Jersey Heritage. I called in to have a word with Jon Carter, its Director since 2003, having been with the Trust since 1989. Jon was educated at Victoria College and Leeds University where he read History. Later he studied for a Master's degree in Museum Studies at Leicester. I had done a bit of previous website homework and I knew that the Trust had responsibility for not only the Jersey Museum but also the Maritime Museum, Mont Orgueil, the Jersey Archive, Elizabeth Castle, Hamptonne, Hougue Bie and a number of historic sites, some of which have fairly recently been developed as holiday lets. I asked Jon to tell me more about the Trust's work. 'We're quite rare in heritage terms in that we are the Island's muscum service, its archive service and its historic buildings service; a holistic approach that allows us some joined-up thinking in our job to protect Jersey's heritage, history and character. We have a staff of about 45 and this expands with seasonal employees to around 80. And I believe that we are very cost-effective: in round terms the States gives us £2m a year and we generate something over £1m in admissions charges and revenue from our commercial activities.'

Jon went further and described the Trust's philosophy: 'We exist to preserve the Island's heritage and not to lay on tourist attractions. But you can't work away at preservation in isolation. That's why our recent forts and towers developments are so important; if these buildings cannot be used, then they will deteriorate. Commercial considerations and preservation are not opposites; you have to generate an audience and capture its interest, and that helps making us some money. And we have to do both of these things to achieve preservation.'

I was reminded that the controversy over the restoration of Mont Orgueil was raging when Jon took over the Trust a few years ago. This was his response to my comments on that hot topic of the time: 'The Mont Orgueil saga was important in that it was a springboard for massive interest in our historic environment. Also increased admission revenues as a result of the restoration have helped to keep our finances healthy. The development of many historic sites followed on. Take Seymour Tower for example; we had 150 people staying out there last year, including guides trained by us taking kids for two-night stays. And there's the radio tower at Corbière: a 95% occupancy through the year and consequent revenue generated to subsidise other restorations.'

There seem to be two gleams in Jon Carter's eye for the future. One of them is Elizabeth Castle. 'Elizabeth Castle is the big challenge. Think about it: the town was founded as a market by the monks from the Castle, the home of our eponymous saint. It is absolutely central to the history of St Helier and has been neglected. There are ten basically empty buildings there, and the challenge to develop the Castle, a hugely significant site, in the right way is powerful.'

The other gleam in the Director's eye is St Helier itself. 'If the Island continues to develop with all the consequent pressures of encroachment on the countryside,

Ordnance Yard

then the town becomes increasingly important in order to counter them. I lived in St Helier for ten years when I returned to the Island; it has some wonderful buildings of real character. This is one of our biggest heritage challenges: to preserve the town's character and to make it again a marvellous place to live. We want more than office and commercial ghettos. And that goes for the Waterfront too: get the appropriate mix of residential, retail and offices.'

Did Jon want to add anything further to our conversation, I enquired. 'No thanks,' he said cheerfully, 'I am relieved to have got all that off my chest.' And with that I left, inspired by his so evident enthusiasm and vision.

~

Round from the Museum and at the bottom of the steps from Pier Road is Ordnance Yard, small surviving enclave of an old St Helier which has been almost completely obliterated. If the presence of rubbish bins is ignored and with the eyes at least half-closed, here is a Dickensian scene of little courtyards with their original granite cobbles and setts. Alas, it is all very seedy and down at heel. Brett suggested over 30 years ago that, if restored, Ordnance Yard could be comparable to The Lanes in Brighton. Sadly the idea was never adopted.

I now crossed the busy dual carriageway at the western end of the tunnel and contemplated the very long range of buildings facing the Old Harbour. A plaque on the wall announced that this was Le Quai des Marchands – or Commercial Buildings as it is now called. Construction was started in 1814 and completed four years later; these stone-fronted terraces of three-storey warehouses, with pink granite of the highest quality, are handsome indeed, except for various ill-considered alterations and additions that have marred the harmony of the range. And that is not my only grouse: Normans, the builders' merchants, occupy many of these buildings and the granite here has been over-painted with a vile, bilious yellow (apparently such a sad choice of colour is outside the remit of the planners). I popped in to the first of these warehouses, the cement store, and caught up with Frank McFarland, in charge behind the counter. He is a Scotsman who has been in the Island for 18 years. Married with a Jersey-born wife and four children, he had been contemplating a return to his native soil and told me this: 'With four kids we've decided to stay in Jersey. It's a lovely place and the schools are good. The problem however is that the Island is expensive.' Frank also told me something about Normans: 'It's the largest firm of this sort in the Island and has been going since 1845. It's been recently taken over by the English firm, Jewsons, and Jewsons itself is owned by a French company called Lafarge. So we're no longer a Jersey business but part of a concern with 200,000 employees and outlets in 52 countries.' Frank seemed unphased by these developments and I finally put to him the 64,000-dollar question: what did he think of the yellow outside? His reply was brief and diplomatic: 'Well, it's a brand.'

~

At the end of Commercial Buildings I took in the sad sight of the boarded-up La Folie Inn on the promontory between the English and the French Harbour and made my way onto South Pier where the premises of the St Helier Yacht Club fit snugly into the red stone warehouses at the end of the quay. I wandered in and encountered Christopher Fairbairn, retired civil servant, member of the Yacht Club since the age of twelve and currently - for a two-year term - its Commodore. He told me that the Club was founded in 1903 and had been in these premises since 1952. 'We took it over after its time as a coal shed during and after the Occupation. We're tenants of Jersey Harbours and in the intervening years have developed it, with its 3,600 members, into one of the nicest yacht clubs in the south of the British Isles.' For what reason did people become members? 'They are sailors or motor-boaters – like-minded people. And we have all the facilities here, teaching yacht safety, navigation, the use of VHF radio and life rafts and so on. People buy a boat and join us to get some basic knowledge and to enjoy the club facilities including the franchised-out bar and catering.'

We were seated on the first floor and looking out north over the Old Harbour with its many small craft moored up and, with the tide out, sitting on the bottom. Christopher told me that this had been the Island's commercial harbour, with the sailing trading ships from all over the world mooring up alongside the walls and the warehouses. 'Is it a good idea having a harbour that dries out?' I asked. 'Actually it was and is a big advantage. In the old days if a ship was aground you could see into the holds, and the boat bottoms could be careened. St Aubin's Harbour got too small when trade burgeoned and the commercial business moved here. Interestingly we have one harbour in Jersey which never dries out and that's St Catherine's; all the other harbours are built on dry land.'

The Commodore is not in favour of tentative plans to flood the Old Harbour by putting a lock-gate in and covering over the fine granite walls with concrete – in order to attract super-yachts, some from the Mediterranean. 'The Club is not in favour; most of the boats here are on cradles and this allows us to scrub the bottoms. And also it's far cheaper for a mooring here than in the fairly new west of Albert marina.'

Christopher finally filled me in on the Yacht Club's plans for the future: 'We're in the process of trying to get our lease extended and then spending £350,000 on this property – re-wiring, re-plumbing, doing the heating and, downstairs, a yachting training centre. We're very comfortable here; it's been our home for sixty years, and we've been representing yachtsmen, training them and keeping them safe at sea.'

St Helier Yacht Club seen across the French Harbour

JOURNEY ROUND St HELIER ~

~

I now headed for La Collette, not St Helier's most picturesque spot and all of it land reclaimed from the sea decades ago. The first building on my left, looking neat and serviceable, was the States abattoir. I wanted to call in and make what would have been for me a first visit to such an establishment, but no one answered the bell on the main door and persons later contacted by phone seemed reluctant to arrange the opportunity for a chat. I moved on and, before heading deeper into this strange industrial landscape, I cast a glance to my left at the power station that provides a back-up facility for Jersey's electricity supply, were France's cabled supply of 'juice' to fail. I decided not to call in; Peter Routier, Jersey Electricity's company secretary and David Killip, the production manager, had given me an extensive tour when a few years back I was preparing my *Journey Round Jersey*, and those curious to know more about the power station's impressive interior with its cathedral-like turbine hall will have to buy or borrow a copy of my earlier book. But a comment is justified about the building itself and its chimney in particular. The modern power station was constructed in 1965 and, though hard to see, is actually tacked on to a considerable range of two-storey stone 18th century government buildings. The enormous chimney, dominating St Helier's and some of the Island's skyline certainly deserves a mention: it is an elongated hexagon that encases within its concrete walls several distinct flues, all of which terminate in a single oversailing lid. Below the top layer is a patterned series of small openings, perhaps - or perhaps not – centrally heated pigeonholes for smoke-loving doves. Its conscious 'design' was presumably a device to disguise its rather stark gracelessness, but many will conclude that the attempt failed.

I turned my back on the power station and crossed the road to Huelin-Renouf's big modern warehouse. In its yard I headed for what seemed an office, entered and was confronted by the backs of four seated men, all of whose attention was concentrated on their computer screens. One turned to me, enquired of my business and, when I replied, directed me to the man at the end of the row. He swivelled round, and there was Terry Amy, known well by me in another context, he being a server at All Saints church in The Parade where on Sundays I play the organ. Terry was just the right man to tell me about Huelin-Renouf Shipping and his own position with the firm. 'I'm the freight office manager and have worked for the company on the Victoria Pier for sixteen years. We're the only people dealing with all the freight – a lift-on/lift-off operation as opposed to Condor which is roll-on/roll-off. We don't deal with the perishable goods; we deal, just for example, with white goods, the toilet rolls, the coffins, soft and fizzy drinks and very much more. Yes, we're Jersey-owned and we have our own ship the Huelin Dispatch that can take 140 units (they're the 20ft containers). It does a three times a week round trip to Portsmouth, and the company is actually having a new ship being built in

~ THE ROYAL SQUARE TO FORT REGENT...

Germany, due here within the year.' Bumping into Terry pretty well every Sunday for the previous three and a half years, I felt guilty at not knowing more about him. He enlightened me: 'I've been involved at All Saints for 54 years, starting Sunday School there when I was six. I'm Jersey-born, received a grammar school education at Hautlieu, worked for Sealink (or British Railways as it was then), then had a spell in the finance industry, joined Huelin-Renouf in 1992 and have been here ever since.' Terry and I then chatted a little about his Jersey life, only being away from the Island for holidays. 'There are a lot worse places; it's a safe environment especially for bringing up children. Yes, it's got a lot busier in the last few years – and more expensive.' And he concluded by telling me a little about his son, daughter-in-law and granddaughter, adding, 'I've got a good number one wife and we've been married 36 years.' It had been a pleasant surprise to bump into an acquaintance; I made my farewells and, as I left, said to Terry, 'See you on Sunday.'

~

Much of La Collette appears to be dominated by its fuel farm and curiosity led me to Fuel Supplies (C.I.) Ltd and the office of its finance director, David Knight, where he and I were joined by the finance manager, Peter Gully. David and Peter are both men born and educated in Jersey. David has been with this Guernsey-registered company for nine years and Peter for a much longer period. Peter filled me in on this big oil depot: 'In the 1970s there was a big fire at the gas company in Town and the fire chief got badly burnt. As a consequence of all this he decided to move the gas company. At the time we were sited at the harbour behind La Folie Inn. So it was agreed to get all the fuel companies out of the way and into one area; hence our move in 1979 to this reclaimed site.'

David told me that the fuel farm was owned jointly by Shell and Esso and that there was a consortium: 'We have Esso fuel coming in and Shell fuel coming in, and the third firm, Total, draws its supplies from Esso.' I also learned that there are three varieties of fuel here: petrol, diesel and kerosene (both the home heating variety and the more refined product that goes to the airport). And the number of fuel tanks? 'There are thirteen,' which, I interjected, hardly seemed a lucky number for an oil depot. 'They are eleven metres high and the very big ones have a capacity of a million litres. We have once-a-week deliveries, with Esso boats coming in from Southampton and Shell boats from Pembroke.'

And how safe was all this? Were we still too near Town? David was quick to say that he had no worries on that score: 'There's a whole raft of safety procedures and manuals for us to observe.' Nor has Peter any concerns: 'I have no sleepless nights either. There is the occasional false alarm when we exit the building quickly. And if for example the alarm goes off now, then we're out.'

JOURNEY ROUND St HELIER ~

Finally I was told that, in all, the three fuel companies operating from here have a total of 30 or so delivery tankers and that plans for the expected development of a big incinerator at La Collette with its energy-from-waste programme should not affect the continued operation of the fuel farm. Peter pithily summed it all up for me: 'Boats bring the fuel in; it goes into the tanks; and it passes from them into lorries and to whoever in the Island wants the products which we supply.'

~

Before leaving this strange corner of St Helier I had two further visits to make – to the headquarters and depot of Jersey's bus provider, Connex Transport Jersey Ltd, and to the reclamation site, fortuitously termed for this area reclaimed from the sea, that occupies a major part of the La Collette peninsula and stretches a considerable distance south. At Connex I climbed the stairs to reception on the first floor of this office block-cum-garage and had a chat with Emily Moore, its marketing manager. Emily described her responsibilities: 'I oversee the network's communications, all the timetables and all the PR contacts with the media. I'm involved with the initial design work for brochures, posters and the other literature that we send out; and I am in charge of customer services and the correspondence which comes in.' She was able to give me a number of facts about Connex's Jersey operations: a fleet of 77 vehicles for the scheduled routes, the school buses and the summer months' Island Explorer service that takes in the bays and the main tourist attractions. A core of permanent full-time drivers is supplemented by both part-time and seasonal staff. And she told me about one of the company's headaches: 'In Jersey there is this width restriction on the vehicles, and we can't just go to the UK and buy buses from another operator. They have to be specially manufactured or sourced very carefully.'

How was Connex going to get me out of my car and into a bus? 'Yes, it is hard to persuade people to leave their cars and use public transport, but we are ever looking at new ideas and contemplating new routes, trying to find the gaps and come up with solutions. Also passenger numbers do go up and up year on year: an above-eleven per cent rise in this last year.'

Finally Emily Moore, dragged by me away from her busy desk for a full quarter of an hour, described what must surely be Connex's jewel in the crown – the recently opened Liberation Station on the Esplanade (already visited by me) that has released the Weighbridge from its sad and long-standing duty as an unsightly bus terminus. 'Liberation Station is a wonderful, state-of-the-art facility: no dangerous mingling of public and buses; passengers waiting under cover; buses entering a tunnel at the back of the building and automatic doors that open when boarding begins. Pop in and see the computer screens and the facilities: more like an airport than a bus station. All this has gone hand in hand with our new text-messaging service: wait at the bus stop, key in to your mobile the code number displayed there and receive the precise information as to where your bus is and when it will arrive.' I felt a degree of guilt as I left the Connex offices and glanced at my car sitting outside and ready to take me home in due course.

~

Only yards from Connex the coming and going of lorries and trucks and two large notices made clear the nature of their destination. The one announced:

> La Collette Reclamation Site
> And Aggregates Recycling Site
> -
> Asbestos Reception Site

The other proclaimed:

> Garden Waste and Packaging Timber Reception

I wandered in to a large, dusty, open area flanked by Portakabins and caught up with the man in charge. I wanted a chat but he was politely reluctant to talk to me: 'It's a political matter and you'll have to seek out someone higher up,' I was told. But he kindly gave me the freedom to wander and I set off south for more than half a mile along a wide unmetalled road. I quickly found myself in an incredible wasteland: high hills of compost emitting a fairly robust odour; mountains of glass (so that's where my wine bottles end up); great piles of tarmac scooped off road surfaces; and much more of what to me was unidentifiable waste of all sorts. Eventually, further out than Elizabeth Castle to the west, I arrived at great boundary walls of granite blocks, containing the land from the sea and enclosing deep ravines waiting to be in-filled. Everywhere large excavators and dumper trucks were busily at work. I turned and tramped the good step back to the site's entrance, denied the opportunity of imparted information but with my interest having been caught by a scenario undisclosed to most.

~

It was now time for me to leave La Collette, hardly the most attractive if nonetheless an essential part of St Helier. I climbed Mount Bingham and descended on its eastern side to Havre Des Pas. To be honest, this part of Town is rather a muddle: tall flats and a large, high, former hotel, now apartments, are jumbled with Regency villas, Victorian guesthouses, modest cottages and more modern, less appealing dwellings. Architectural charms, from the period after 1824 when a regular steamboat service from England to Jersey brought holiday-makers requiring accommodation, are still just visible; perhaps it is to be regretted that imaginative plans, including a big marina, of two decades ago, were never adopted. If it is an area that, in Brett's words, 'has got out of hand', then a fresh and radical development could have been beneficial.

Three Havre des Pas buildings, however, deserved my particular attention. The first is the seawater bathing pool, flooded at the high tides, which, after many years of indecision and discussion, opened in 1895, surely a complementary addition to what must have then been a fine Victorian resort and possibly one of the earliest lidos and the only one in the British Isles to be surrounded by water. Its heyday as a swimming centre was in the 1920s and 1930s. After 1971, when the Fort Regent indoor pool opened, its fortunes unsurprisingly declined and, a few years ago, an architects' report described it as lying 'decaying like a scuppered ship'. Since then it has been handsomely restored and continues to fulfil something of its original, more than century-old, function. The person who both knows all about the pool and indeed who uses it regularly is Angie Boucheré, Fort Regent's centre manager. In her office there she told me about its history and its recent restoration. 'We have a supervisor and lifeguards in the summer and it's open from the end of May till the end of September; and there's no admission charge – it's free swimming; perhaps 200 to 300 people a day.' Angie went on to tell me about the 'polar bears'. 'There are about 40 of them who swim there every day all the year round, no matter what the weather.' And she let on that she's something of a polar bear herself: 'I swim there every Saturday and Sunday throughout the year.' I shivered slightly as I bade her farewell.

~

Further along from the pool and on the north side of the road is the Ommaroo Hotel. It actually consists of several tall Victorian seafront houses, and Brett's description of it is worth my quoting in full: 'Part stone, part stucco, with astonishing frilly and lacy fretted balconies, railings and barge-boards, some of wood, some of iron, as seductive as a demi-mondaine's underwear'. It is just a pity that the doubtless necessary modern hotel conservatory intrudes on this distinctive frontage, constituting at least a slight sartorial blemish.

Across the road from the Ommaroo is a house appropriately named Petit Chateau de la Mer. Again Brett is to the point if, for these days, politically incorrect. Here is his description of this beguiling villa: 'A charming mixture of froggy styles, with a square turret on top of stucco arcading'. (He even failed to put inverted commas round what might by some be considered an offensive adjective.)

I retraced my steps towards Town and made for the States offices of Planning

Havre Des Pas house

and Building at South Hill. (It is surely a pity that our Island planners are housed in such an unprepossessing post-war block; a more handsome headquarters might perhaps give its civil servants added assurance and enthusiasm for their undoubtedly heavy, environmentally important and sometimes controversial duties.) I had an appointment with the Minister responsible, Senator Freddie Cohen, who welcomed me warmly into his cluttered office. I first wanted to know what he had done before being elected to the States in 2005. He replied: 'I was a property developer in Jersey and elsewhere until I lost interest eight or nine years ago. Since then I have written a couple of books – on the Occupation – and worked with Jersey Heritage Trust in an honorary capacity on a number of schemes.' His appointment as Environment Minister came on his first day in the States and I asked him about what must have been a baptism of fire. 'I found myself on day one not knowing about politics, new (like everyone else) to the experience of being a minister and with no chief officer at the department which had been split. But I rapidly realised that the States Planning Department could deliver more than it was doing and that what the Island needed were good buildings. When I was a developer here I built in the Jersey vernacular. In fact it's easier that way: local stone, local proportion windows and arches. Take Brittany, St Peter Port, the Cotswolds, Bath: the buildings that emerge in the prevalent style are the ones most comfortable for those environments. Jersey has ignored this and over the years has produced too much inferior architecture. Of recent developments Morier House, the Jersey Archive and the West Park apartments are three fairly rare exceptions.'

It could not have surprised Senator Cohen that I, as the author of *Hotel, West of Albert: Jersey's Waterfront Saga* published in 2001, would want to ask him about the Waterfront and his plans for it. 'It is the most important challenge for the Island. Everything that we have seen there so far is frankly awful. I scrapped the current proposals and want to deliver something of architectural excellence; hence the appointments of leading architect Sir Michael Hopkins and one of the world's experts in landscaping, Robert Townshend. We are dealing with plans for a mix of offices, three hundred residences and four public squares, using the highest quality of materials including granite masonry. Some people are naturally very cautious about this Hopkins master plan, but I believe that, if I can get it through the States, we shall be delivering an inspiring vision for future generations.'

And what about creeping development into the countryside? 'We should in principle have a moratorium against any building there. What is Jersey's image? It is countryside, cows, small fields, granite farms. To preserve this we have got to come up with some radical responses. People's aspirations for a house and garden in a rural parish must change; we have to make the town a better place to live in. Think of the former elegance of St Helier's early 19th century villas and crescents; and consider their current multi-occupancy, poor renovation and so on. Town requires re-investment with people proud to live there. We have a long task ahead of us making Jersey people aspire to being urban dwellers. And that leads us back to the Waterfront, because it is the Waterfront that can create the catalyst for that change.'

The next meeting in the Minister's diary beckoned and I had only a few minutes to lob two other balls in his direction – Plémont and ministerial government. As to the first, Senator Cohen was explicit: 'Plémont should be returned to the public; it should be open to all of us and not have houses built on it.' I was then told how Plémont's developer had a case for consent being given him and, after that process had been determined, then the States should purchase the area. As to ministerial government having succeeded the former committee system, he was not unexpectedly enthusiastic: 'I am privileged to be in the position of being able to deliver my dream of better architecture for Jersey. As a Minister I have the tools significantly to improve the quality of the Island's buildings and you will see this coming through steadily over the years ahead. As to the ministerial system in general, I think there is a need to restructure the process in one key area: the Chief Minister should have considerably more powers than he has at present.' With that I gave my thanks and made my farewells, wondering as I left whether I had been talking with one who might himself one day occupy that top position in the Island's government.

~

I turned right out of the South Hill offices and climbed up towards Fort Regent. Now at times in the last few years there have been voices raised that St Helier needs an iconic building. This sentiment surely fails to embrace the fact that the town already possesses two of them – Elizabeth Castle and Fort Regent. Indeed the Fort, from its redevelopment of the late 1960s with its dome (perhaps looking back to the 1951 Festival of Britain rather than forward) and now redundant swimming pool, is a dominant if controversial feature of St Helier's skyline. This extensive and solid fortification was built between 1806 and 1814. Commanding the harbour from its steep rocky outcrop and with its well-squared and dressed granite, it was occupied by units of the British army until 1927, sold to the States of Jersey in 1958 and then developed as a leisure centre nearly forty years ago. (A word should be said about the former swimming pool, completed in 1971 and poorly sited and an unduly bulky intrusion on the Fort's glacis field.) Over these past decades some would question whether Fort Regent has ever really found a proper role. I called on its centre manager, Angie Boucheré, our Havre des Pas weekend 'polar bear', Jersey-born and involved in its administration for 37 years, to tell me more.

Angie summed up the Fort's current purpose: 'For all these years it's been both an entertainment and a sports venue. Yes, the fairground attractions, the crazy golf, the piazza activities have gone, but the rooms round the side are used for martial arts and the play area for children is the largest in the Island. And we have a huge, big gym and over 4,000 members. Also there are lots of shows, concerts and events in the Gloucester and Queen's halls. We've got the Kenpo Karate world championships soon and hundreds will be attracted to them. There are also the performances – the big entertainment names and the Jersey Symphony Orchestra concerts for example.'

View across St Helier rooftops towards Fort Regent

I pitched at Angie Boucheré an oft-debated question: what of the Fort's future, a topic frequently brought up by the politicians? In reply the centre manager told me that reports were always being commissioned from consultants and investment was sometimes promised – perhaps a fast lift from Snow Hill, possibly a new use for the former swimming pool. But despite uncertainties, she spoke confidently about its current function: 'We have at least 400,000 visits a year. With our sports activities, visitors from the mainland marvel at the excellence of our facilities. And if another use were found for the Fort, then the States would have to make provision for all the sports elsewhere. The fact is that everyone who uses the Fort loves it.'

~

~ THE ROYAL SQUARE TO FORT REGENT...

As I bade farewell to Angie she invited me to take a solitary wander round this remarkable place. At one point I saw on the walls a series of photographs. One of them captured the depressing picture of the Fort's great parade ground being used in the post-war period, and before developments started at the end of the 1960s, as a coal depot and general dumping ground. Fort Regent today is surely an improvement on that. But I have to admit to a sense of depression as I strode across what had once been a huge early 19th century parade ground with its fine surrounding granite buildings but now covered over by a dome and filled by the no doubt ingeniously constructed modern halls. This was the thought that crossed my mind: should possibly another purpose have been found four decades ago, more faithfully preserving the Fort's history and structure, for what was once such an original and impressively sited military fortification, now almost 200 years old?

With these considerations in mind I descended through the car park to Pier Road and made my way slowly back to the Royal Square where my journey round St Helier had started.

Also by Robin Pittman and published by Seaflower Books:

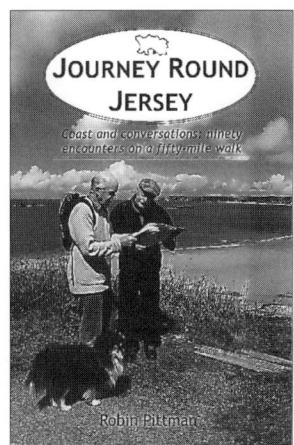
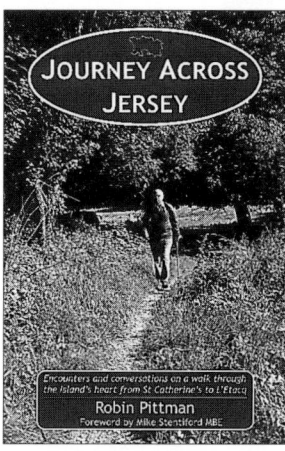

JOURNEY ROUND JERSEY:
Coast and conversations: ninety encounters on a fity-mile walk
ISBN 1-903341-28-0;
176 pages; £7.95

JOURNEY ACROSS JERSEY: Encounters and conversations on a walk through the island's heart from St Catherine's to L'Etacq
ISBN 978-1-903341-44-5;
96 pages; £5.95

SPEAKING OF JERSEY: Reflections on the Island's Past, Present and Future
ISBN 1-903341-14-0;
224 pages; £7.95

More titles from Seaflower Books are as follows:

JERSEY: NOT QUITE BRITISH: The Rural History of a Singular People
by David Le Feuvre
Absorbing account of Jersey's rural heritage.
ISBN 1 903341 27 2; 160 pages; £6.95

CHANNEL FISH: A Book of Fish Cookery from the Channel Islands
by Marguerite Paul
Our bestselling fish cookery book.
ISBN 0 903341 10 8; 24 pages; £9.95

ISLAND KITCHEN: A Book of Seasonal Cookery from the Channel Islands
by Marguerite Paul
Follow-up to 'Channel Fish', featuring seasonal produce, local and not-so-local recipes.
ISBN 0 903341 18 3; 192 pages; £9.95

JERSEY HORSES FROM THE PAST
by John Jean
Pictorial presentation of the vital role our four-legged friends once played.
ISBN 0 903341 01 9; 96 pages; £4.95

WILD ISLAND: Jersey Nature Diary
by Peter Double
The natural year in Jersey, profusely and beautifully illustrated.
ISBN 0 948578 77 7; 120 pages; £7.95

WILDLIFE OF THE CHANNEL ISLANDS
by Sue Daly
A beautiful and informative book featuring some 240 superb photographs in full-colour.
ISBN 1 903341 24 8; 221 pages; £14.95

BLAME THE BADGER for a Wild Life!
by Mike Stentiford, MBE
The popular Jersey naturalist tells his story.
ISBN 978-1-906641-05-4; 144 pages; £6.95

EXOTIC GARDEN PLANTS IN THE CHANNEL ISLANDS
by Janine Le Pivert
Illustrated throughout in full colour
ISBN 978-1-903341-40-7; 128 pages; £9.95

ISLAND DESTINY
A true story of love and war in the Channel Island of Sark
by Richard Le Tissier
The inspiring story of Werner Rang, a member of the German occupying forces, who eventually married a local woman and settled happily in the island.
ISBN 1-903341-36-1' 160 pages; £6.95

LIFE ON SARK by Jennifer Cochrane
Tells what it is like to live throughout the year on the Channel Island with the greatest mystique.
ISBN 0 948578 63 7   128 pages; £5.95

MINED WHERE YOU WALK
The German Occupation of Sark, 1940-45
by Richard Le Tissier
The first proper record of the five years of Occupation in Sark.
ISBN 978-1-906641-00-9;142 pages; £6.95

PRISON WITHOUT BARS: Living in Jersey under the German Occupation, 1940-45
by Frank Keiller
Growing up as a teenager during the Occupation. Exciting stuff!
ISBN 1 903341 00 0; 192 pages; £6.95

GUERNSEY COUNTRY DIARY: Through the Natural Year with Nigel Jee
Informative, amusing and altogether delightful account of the natural year in Guernsey.
ISBN 0 948578 90 4; 128 pages; £4.95

JERSEY WITCHES, GHOSTS & TRADITIONS
by Sonia Hillsdon
Ghoulies, ghosties and things that go bump in the night!
ISBN 1 903341 13 2; 160 pages; £6.50

THE JERSEY LILY: The Life and Times of Lillie Langtry
by Sonia Hillsdon
Our second bestselling title.
ISBN 0 948578 55 6; 128 pages; £5.95

JERSEY OCCUPATION DIARY: Her Story of the German Occupation 1940-45
by Nan Le Ruez
First-hand account of one Jerseywoman's experience of the Occupation. Riveting reading.
ISBN 1 903341 19 1; 240 pages; £9.95

JERSEY OCCUPATION REMEMBERED
by Sonia Hillsdon
The Occupation experience, in the words of those who lived through it.
ISBN 1 903341 213; 160 pages; £5.95

JERSEY RAMBLES: Coast and Country
by John Le Dain
Latest edition of our perennial bestseller features new Jersey Coast-to-Coast walk.
ISBN 1 904431 26 4   128 pages; £5.95

JERSEY JAUNTS
33 Circular Walks with Refreshments
by John Le Dain
Short(ish) walks, all new, exploring various corners of the island, many of which are little visited
ISBN 978-1-903341-41-4; 80 pages; £5.95

JERSEY WEATHER AND TIDES
by Peter Manton
Jersey's weather sets records in the UK and its tides are some of the world's biggest. Learn more from this book.
ISBN 0 948578 75 0; 96 pages; £5.95

JOHN SKINNER'S VISIT TO THE CHANNEL ISLANDS: August 1827
Edited by John Le Dain
Revealing journal of a short-break tourist to Guernsey and Jersey in 1827.
ISBN 1 903341 25 6; 20 pages; £2.50

WISH YOU WERE HERE…
A Holiday History of Jersey seen through picture postcards
by John Le Dain
More than 250 Jersey postcards, many with holiday messages, from the 1900s to the 1960s.
ISBN 1 903341 12 4; 192 pages; £9.95

Seaflower Books are available through your local bookshop, via Amazon, or may be obtained direct from the publisher, post-free, via the website

SEAFLOWER BOOKS

www.ex-librisbooks.co.uk

16A New St John's Road
St Helier
Jersey   JE2 3LD